Col. Michael Edward Masters'

Hospitality – Kentucky Style

Simply Elegant Cooking and Entertaining

Library of Congress Catalog Number - 2001116697

Design and type formatting by Ken Distler, Digi-Pic Graphics

Equine Writer's Press
P.O. Box 1101
Bardstown, Kentucky 40004

Printed in the United States of America

Table Of Contents

Acknowledgments

The home in which I was raised was one of Southern grace and warm Kentucky gentility. My appreciation for cooking fine foods and entertaining on a grand scale came from my father, Dr. V. Edward Masters, and my mother, Barbara Gallagher Masters, both extraordinary hosts at their home, Elmwood. In their home, celebrating life has been an everyday event.

Many of the recipes you will find in my entertaining originated in my mother's kitchen and many others have her influence. When I was growing up no one wanted to go out to eat, they wanted my mother, known to all as Mimi, to cook for them. Being in the home of my father and mother, surrounded by family and friends, enjoying good Kentucky bourbon with a regal dinner upon the sideboard, are some of my fondest memories. The essence of this graceful Kentucky heritage, I hope, I have conveyed to you in this book.

I wish to acknowledge my wife, Margaret Sue, her grandmother whom we call Mama Sudie, and her mother Sue Carol, for their contributions to my life and the influence they have had on my cooking. Their family home, Holloway House, has been the setting for exquisite entertaining. All three of these women have been fantastic cooks of Kentucky cuisine and wonderful hostesses.

Allow me to give my wife, Margaret Sue an especial acknowledgment. Margaret Sue's sense of style, Southern manners and ways, as passed to her from her grandmother and mother, have been a joy to me, immeasurable. Margaret Sue can pull together a party at our home, McManus House in Bardstown, Kentucky, for ten or two hundred. She makes it appear effortless. And when she summons Mimi, Sue Carol and other family and friends, who always appear on the scene to help, I believe they could build a house in a day if they chose to.

To my sisters Alice Carolyn and Martha Barbara; and my children Colin and Carolyn— I am eternally grateful to them for their affection, their Kentucky charm and the loving support they have always granted me. To all of my family and friends — you are an integral part of this book.

To Larry and Mary Ellyn Hamilton, Ramona McKinney, Michael Embry, Harry Sherrard, David Ballard, Julie McRay Waits, Ginny Roby—thank you for proof reading my original drafts.

To Margaret Sue, Mary Ellyn Hamilton and Julie McRay Waits, thank you for your assistance in helping develop the image I wanted to create for this book.

I am grateful to Ken Hoskins, an extraordinary public relations mind, and to Stephen Vest, the publisher of *Kentucky Monthly,* for their editorial advice.

I am deeply grateful to John Neil, the wonderful artist who created the line drawings of our Kentucky homes. John and his wife, Ruth, have encouraged me every step along my journey with this book.

Thanks to John Bramel for his incredible cover photograph.

To C.R. Barnes, whom I never had the pleasure of meeting, but whose life is an inspiration to me.

And to a man in Bardstown, Kentucky who requests anonymity—he is a man who has challenged and encouraged me to create my dream. I say, with all the sincerity I can muster, thank you.

I have used selected writings from *All That's Kentucky*, 1915 edited by Josiah H. Combs, an anthology, that my research shows to be out of copyright and in the public domain. It is poetry and prose that I have admired for years and by including it in this book, it is my hope that I can help preserve some of it.

And lastly, when I give a toast at the dining table, as everyone at the table knows I will, I raise my glass to my family and friends, to the women in my life—beauties one and all—and to Kentucky!

Colonel Michael Edward Masters
McManus House
Bardstown, Kentucky

The Kentucky Gentleman

Gentlemen in Kentucky have often been considered good cooks and hosts. The Kentucky gentleman is a competent cook for the recipes he has embraced, be that a recipe for food or libation. The Kentucky gentleman knows how to make guests to his home feel welcome. He knows by tradition that his role is to charm the women and children, prepare the foods that are associated with him and to tend an excellent bar.

It is a common experience in Kentucky to join your host at breakfast, after an overnight stay in his family's home, to be pleasingly surprised that he is baking you his signature breakfast biscuit or baked cheese grits. The family will heap fond praise upon this gentleman as encouragement and to see once again, the pride with which he offers his breakfast to those assembled. And you will find, if you have an extended stay, that at every meal he prepares one or two of his recipes.

Kentucky gentlemen, polite men of a chivalrous and generous nature, enjoy the privilege of cooking for their family and friends. This is not to say that the foods they prepare are of an intricate nature requiring a great deal of time and forethought. To the contrary, a Kentucky gentleman in the kitchen has recipes that he finds are within his ability to make and that when he presents them at table will bring him rave reviews.

When Margaret Sue and I entertain, many in our extended family prepare the foods that we glowingly acknowledge are their specialty and they bring them over. Everyone looks forward to Margaret Sue's pimento cheese, Mama Sudie's yeast rolls, Mimi's chocolate sauce, Sue Carol's Benedictine and the Colonel's Beef Masters. On my word I could do it all, but we would all miss the convivial spirit of a contributed specialty. Praise, in my world, has an infinite quality.

In the modern day it is important that we make time for the people with whom we choose to share our lives. We make every attempt to celebrate not only the birthdays and the holidays but also seek ways to enjoy the seasons. In our fast paced world we all too often have our children, our parents, sisters, brothers, cousins and old friends living along every point on the globe.

Kentucky is known worldwide for gracious hospitality. We speak of old friends as being a part of our family; and we hold the out-of-town guests of our friends in the same high regard we hold the friends they are visiting. On our table is the Kentucky cuisine our friends and out of town guests remember lovingly for the rest of their lives. On our bar is stocked the bourbon we consider the finest, in our opinion.

I have read most of the cookbooks that professional writers have published about Kentucky cuisine. My observation has been that the recipes they offer, often, are of a different time. Few people today are going to find any food preparation process attractive that involves intense labor and an extraordinary level of cooking skill to achieve superlative results.

If I have a second observation, it is that many writers do not entertain in their home and therefore tend to report recipes and ways of doing things that were related to them by professional chefs and catering concerns. I have read books about cooking that would require a dozen staff and multiple layers of editors to bring them to press.

I do not claim to be a chef, this title being reserved for cooks of formal training and possessing an academic background in the chemistry and art of food preparation. I rely upon my experience as a host and the training I have received from numerous family and friends, many of whom were exceptionally good Kentucky cooks who had great flair in their entertaining. The fact that I was a vice president of a large regional restaurant chain, no doubt, also had a considerable influence on me.

You will notice that I accommodate modern sensibilities and wherever possible I use food combinations to sweeten and season the foods I cook. When I err from the past, it is usually on the side of olive oil, lemon and ground pepper. In this collection you will find recipes that are traditional to Kentucky and are easily prepared by anyone who enjoys cooking. I leave the complex recipes to others who have gourmet training.

I have selected the entrées, vegetables, dressings, sauces, breads, salads and desserts that I know are simply great. You do not need many signature recipes to be acknowledged as an excellent cook. The recipes I enjoy are ones that I can prepare ahead of time or are simple enough to put together while I socialize with everyone, all of whom crowd into the kitchen—although there are another eight rooms in the house.

In our entertaining at McManus House, it is characteristic to our style that we embrace recipes that can be prepared either a few hours or a day ahead of our party. Our way is to enjoy the people in our lives and to welcome them into our home. We have no intention of becoming slaves to the kitchen while the drinks are being poured!

The elegance that characterizes our social occasions is not based upon lavish entertaining spending but it is in the beautiful presentation of our dining table and bar, and the welcoming warmth of our homes. I offer you my recipes and our way of entertaining in the spirit of *Hospitality – Kentucky Style.*

My Kentucky

The social season in Kentucky extends throughout the year. It is in keeping with our hospitable nature to perceive each season as an opportunity to entertain our family and friends. In our house no distinction is made between the friends we grew up with and the friends we spend time with now. Of course we celebrate all of the usual passages occurring throughout the year. But we also find the passing seasons in Kentucky as a time for entertainment.

The Spring Thoroughbred Meet

The spring horse racing season is a magical time in Kentucky, a time when we invite those "near and dear" to our home with a two-century old unspoken invitation to bring your out-of-town guests. It is a time when the sons and daughters of Kentucky, living in foreign states and lands, feel nostalgic for the home they have left behind. The Stephen Foster song "My Old Kentucky Home" evokes memories of the times in their past, of the family and friends that remain and of those that have departed this life. It is also a time of joyous reunion with our extended family and the friends we hold dear.

Keeneland Race Course in Lexington is the most beautiful racetrack in America. It is here Kentucky-bred Thoroughbred race horses find their shrine. The Keeneland sales in the summer and fall draw the great wealth of the world to this legendary racing establishment to bid on the blood stock sired on the historic horse farms in central Kentucky. The Keeneland sale barns house two hundred years of winning bloodlines. In the spirited auctions, millions of dollars will be spent on the one single hope that, this horse, from the champion bloodstock of his ancestors, standing alone in the sales ring, in their time, will outrun the great Thoroughbred horses of the world and capture fortunes of gold and glory.

We make our pilgrimage to Keeneland Race Course for the spring meeting in April with the anticipation that we will spend the afternoon with the most celebrated horse racing stock upon the globe. Many of the horses will be running their maiden race as two year olds, fresh from the training stables of their central Kentucky farms. Keeneland Race Course is a small racing plant, and was built for the showcasing of Kentucky Thoroughbreds.

The barns and the hot walking arena are in front of the clubhouse and a white boarded fence is all that separates the Keeneland patrons and the horses. The owners and trainers walk their prized horseflesh in front of you, preparing them for the race. The jockeys, many of them the most famous names in horse racing, mount within your view. Whether we elect to watch the race from the elegant clubhouse or at the rail is almost unimportant. It is the horse we are there to see. Racing fans, groomsmen, trainers and owners all stand shoulder to shoulder, equal in their appreciation of the horse, feeling proud to be at Keeneland Race Course, watching the Thoroughbreds run.

Then it is to Churchill Downs we go for the week of racing that precedes the Kentucky Derby, held on the first Saturday in May in Louisville. And it is the time that McManus House sets to work in earnest on the Kentucky breakfast and the Derby party we will host on the lawn.

Every year, as I prepare for our Derby party, I hear from friends about the Derby party they are hosting at their homes in New York, San Francisco, London and other ports of call. The Kentucky Derby will last two minutes, the feelings that the race engenders last all year in the Kentucky heart, whether they reside comfortably in their Kentucky home or find themselves "far, far away."

A Kentucky woman, in this man's opinion, never looks better than she does on Derby Day. There is an excitement in the air that fills the senses—whether going to the track, going to someone's house for a Derby party, going to the club, or the tavern, or to your house where this year "we're just having some of the neighbors over to watch the race." The women find resplendent hats for the Derby: if in a box seat at the track—elegant, broad-brimmed and generously decorated with feathers and flowers; if standing in the infield—broad-brimmed but more on the sun protection survival side; if going to or having a party—then the hat spans the spectrum.

The Kentucky Derby is an international sporting event. The entire Commonwealth is caught up in the high spirit and the women know that the colorful and fashionable presentation of their dress is part and parcel of the human and equine pageantry that is Derby. Men have a role too—to serve the women, to provide the transportation and to enjoy the charm and romance of the Derby week.

For as it is written, so it is indeed:

"If you haven't been to the Derby, you ain't been nowhere and you ain't done nothin." —**Irvin Cobb**

Kentucky Breakfast

When a breakfast is declared and invitations are received in the mail, you are alerted to the fact that you are invited to a very elegant party. Casual dress is implied but to meet the breakfast head on one must remember that casual dress in Kentucky means sporting attire: blazer and ties for the gentlemen and colorful sun dresses and broad-brimmed hats for the gentlewomen. The breakfast gains a special prominence during the spring horse-racing season that begins with visits to Keeneland Race Course in Lexington during the last two weeks of April and concludes at McManus House with the running of the Kentucky Derby held in Louisville on the first Saturday in May.

The breakfast on Derby day is a meal that is an event. Weather permitting, we serve the breakfast on the lawn with seating for all of the guests in attendance at tables draped in white linen with vases of fresh flowers as centerpieces.

Our bar is stocked with orange, tomato and cranberry juices and the liquors that complement them. Two coffees are offered, usually French Roast for those bracing it with a fine aged Kentucky bourbon whisky and a more tepid blend. A good violin, cello or harp is heard playing off to the side.

The buffet table is a sight to behold.

For the entrées we serve turkey hash or creamed chicken Louisville on wild rice in chafing dishes, rows of rare beef tenderloin on silver platters and mounds of Country ham on beaten biscuit and angel biscuits. Hellmann's mayonnaise, Durkee's dressing and Masters Steak Sauce are in view.

Scrambled eggs garnished with chopped parsley and paprika in chafing dishes complement the entrées.

Marinated asparagus and peeled tomatoes with a side dressing of smearcase layered on silver platters set upon ice are the cold vegetables; green beans and baked cheese grits steaming hot in chafing dishes, are the warm vegetables.

Chilled cantaloupe, pineapple and honeydew mixed with strawberry, blackberry and blueberry served in an oversized bowl are the fruit.

Bourbon balls, lemon squares and Kentucky pecan pie are dessert.

The breakfast is served at ten in the morning, and is completed by eleven-thirty, when those going to the track depart. Those remaining will make themselves comfortable, drinking their preference. The signal that the breakfast is at a proper conclusion is when the bar is packed up and the bartender leaves the property, about two o'clock. A close contingency of guests will find their best seat in the McManus House living room, to watch the race at five-thirty. We will dine on Beef Masters at seven in the evening, feeding the elated, weary, sun-baked gang who went to the track, and have returned to us exhausted, but full of testimony about their experiences at Churchill Downs and the Kentucky Derby.

Summer Weddings

I would not like to miss a wedding. If I am graced with an invitation, it is my pleasure to be in attendance. I cannot imagine a party that is more fun than a wedding. Have I ever been to a bad one? Never.

Certainly, there is a considerable range in the opulence. And to be sure, the length of the guest list is determined by the money in the purse. But, regardless of the size of the venture, the reason for the gathering is the same—to bless and to record a marriage of two people in love. The feeling of hope for the future and the promise of lifelong companionship is in full evidence. The more seasoned married couples find their partners hand, remembering their time before the altar; the younger adults are apprehensive knowing their time is near. After the nuptial rite has found a conclusion, the revelry begins.

My friends know how to provide for their guests. They engage their club, reserve the ballroom of a great hotel or employ a brand name catering concern to erect tents on their lawn, having the buffet repast transported to them. In all three cases, they have given the proper instructions to the management. There is a bountiful table or two of the traditional foods known and respected in Kentucky, along with great silver bowls of shrimp, oysters on the half shell, and salmon filet, all beautifully arranged on beds of ice.

When Margaret Sue and I married, I wanted to throw a party at our reception that was so hot it sizzled. And it did, until three in the morning. Since we had invited four hundred guests and were nervous about the weather, we decided to relieve at least some of the stress and anxiety of the day and let my club stage the event. The club was in fine form, resplendent with flowers and garlands of ivy throughout the ballroom. There was a band with five horns, three bars and a table overflowing with food. Glad I did it, had the time of my life, and I have no desire to do it again.

There are other ways to traverse the reception ground. Margaret Sue maintains that my joy in entertaining comes from my doing it, not having it done for me. As always, she is right, even when I protest with all my vigor, to soften my feeling that once again, she has called the shot. A month after we had spent a small fortune on our wedding reception, we summoned together our close family and our best friends and held a second reception on the lawn at McManus House. We had a well stocked bar, our favorite bartender, and a loaded buffet table, accompanied by a good quartet. Saints preserve me—this is just the way I like it.

Margaret Sue's grandmother, Mama Sudie, lived more than

sixty years at Holloway House, her 1840's farmhouse of 10,000 square feet in central Kentucky. Mama Sudie was so beautiful and so elegant in her unassuming style. She hosted over a hundred weddings in that house. She taught school for forty years, and the girls who had enjoyed school outings to Holloway House dreamed of descending her three-story spiral staircase on their wedding day. It was her pleasure to oblige.

The reception for her girls on these occasions was simple. Mama Sudie baked pies and cakes and served coffee and a fruit punch. Mama Sudie did not indulge in the drinking of spirit beverages, though she always kept bourbon in the pantry for cooking. That was her story and she stuck with it. Gentlemen mixed their drink on a table reserved for that purpose on the brick walk on the side of the house. Those were grand times. I wish I could have been at every one.

There is a tradition in Kentucky of hosting a party for your friends who are soon to be wed. In the time in which we live, there does not appear to be a standard age for this blessed event, the age of the betrothed covers a good bit of the human life span and some have had several cracks at it. At McManus House we are very non-judgmental and present a well turned out table for all of the generations and try to stay out of the politics of the matter.

When a large contingency of guests is to be entertained at McManus House we use the pick up foods strategy. However, a small wedding party of fifteen guests or fewer at McManus House calls for rare beef tenderloin. We complement the tenderloin with Country ham slices on angel biscuits, baked cheese grits, asparagus with cheese sauce, a Bibb lettuce salad with vinaigrette, yeast rolls and a dessert that includes anything as long as it is topped with chocolate sauce or bourbon sauce.

Margaret Sue can be counted on to find just the right gift for the bride, leaning heavily toward ceramic bowls that have multiple everyday uses. Sharing a dinner of rare beef tenderloin is my contribution.

Funerals and the Visitation Thereto

I do not like attending funerals. It makes me reflect too closely on life's only inevitability, namely my eventual demise. My more enlightened friends have become comfortable with the passing stages of their life and they articulate a soothing message of life everlasting and hope eternal as they anchor themselves firmly to the rock of their spiritual salvation. I know that these fortunate friends of mine have achieved a higher level of understanding than my own. All I can tell you is, that the inner peace that comforts them, has eluded me. I intend to go out in full battle gear.

Having dispensed with the dark side of the thing, let me tell you that in Kentucky we know how to send the dear departed to their reward. We throw a party. As a matter of fact we throw a number of parties, all designed to comfort the more grief stricken and to celebrate the life taken from those of us still standing.

Nothing brings the Kentucky clans together like the prospect of a visitation. Three days prior to the service, close family become paragons of industry. The more meticulous housekeepers move directly to food preparation. Those who have scarcely hit a lick on their house throughout the year, spring into concerted action to make their home presentable, for family and friends are coming to town.

No other singular life experience has the power of a visitation to heal broken and estranged family relationships, bring back the long-lost cousins and to rekindle old friendships that fell out decades before over an issue now forgotten. And so the word goes out by telephone to a dozen key people that the clan is gatherin' and these in turn contact other key people. This continues until almost everyone who might care has been contacted, all within the space of an hour. The miracle of a Kentucky homecoming is about to unfold.

Knowing that certain houses within the bereaved family will be hit hardest by out of town friends and relations, the food deliveries begin. Platters of sliced Country ham, roast beef and turkey and baskets of rolls and condiments are the first victuals to arrive. Second on the scene is the pimento cheese,

Benedictine, and pecan chicken salad. Lastly, come the cakes and pies, as their preparation required lead time. The host house provides the bar and any help that may be required.

Mama Sudie felt the weight of her duty and made every attempt to get to every place the family groups in her life congregated over the three-day visitation period. She came to several of my family's visitations, never missing a house. She knew very few of the out of town people but was not deterred. She came prepared, wearing her best silk dress, her treasured ivory brooches and silver jewelry. Never one to shirk a task at hand, she always donated a car full of cakes, pies and vegetable casseroles. Mama Sudie liked to get to the place of visitation early, so she could get a good seat, to hold court with the family in question. Mama Sudie did not want to miss an opportunity for folks to meet her.

I have borne witness to so many touching reunions of relations, and the mending of friendship fences at these visitations. The power of showing up to salute the passing of one of our own allows us to appreciate our own life.

I promise you, if I catch you grieving for my passing I will call a Kentucky hant down upon you. Give me a swell party, host a homecoming, recount the fine times we have shared and give me a good toast. I assure you, I have enjoyed every moment of my time being with you.

Standardbred Harness Racing

There are certain immutable truths that I have discovered. One is that, to have a friend, you must be a friend. Another truth, closely related, is that, if you have a friend, you must accept them as they are, bad eye and all.

It is this way with the Kentucky summer. The other three seasons we extol in rhyme and verse but I tell you straight – our summers are hot, humid and devoid of wind and rain. And let there be no doubt about it – this is just the way we like it.

The Kentucky sweltering summer having been noted, allow me to pronounce that Margaret Sue and I embrace our long hot summer. For it is the time we enjoy Standardbred racing. The Thoroughbred, sleek, high strung, with a long lengthy stride, is all about galloping speed. The Standardbred, on the other hand, is steady of nerve and physically compact with well-developed shoulders for front-end propulsion. The Standardbred is an outstanding breed of horse for the quick diagonal trotting and lateral pacing gaits.

Margaret Sue and I start our summer with several visits to The Red Mile in Lexington. The Red Mile features world-class harness racing in the trotting style. We watch the harness races throughout May and June in the comfortable confine of the glass-enclosed clubhouse. We often return to the Red Mile in September to watch the running of the Kentucky Futurity, the oldest harness race in the country, first run in 1893 and one of the three legs of the trotting Triple Crown. The fact that Margaret Sue and I tend to have good luck at The Red Mile parimutual betting window is an additional delight.

The cuisine in the dining room at The Red Mile is regionally renowned. The dinner is served buffet style and sports rare prime rib of beef, shrimp and crab legs on ice, beautifully steamed vegetables and a dessert selection second to no other. Watching harness racing at the Red Mile, dining on their sumptuous repast, drinking a fine aged Kentucky bourbon whisky or a gin Alexander is a wonderful way to commune with the Standardbred horse.

American Saddlebred Horse Shows

Then, throughout the summer, Margaret Sue and I enter the non-betting, highly competitive world of the Kentucky county fair championship horse shows. The American Saddlebred with a high stepping leg movement, characteristic to the breed, dominates these events. The horses trained to compete in five-gaited, three-gaited or pleasure class will be on review, to be judged by the omnipotent show officials standing solemnly in the middle of the arena.

The riders up on these truly American horses range in age from eight to eighty, seek a commanding presence and are dressed to a stylized perfection. The American Saddlebred show horses are trained to a competitive razor's edge, and are groomed impeccably. There is bloom in the bearing of the riders and the horses that reflect their intense desire to win. The warrior partnership of rider and horse enter the show ring, to join the other combatants. The battle to win a first place ribbon is the prize.

The county fair show ring can be as simple as a four-board white fence, encircling the arena with a rural crowd of fairgoers pressed against it. Alternately, the arena can be a great show pavilion, with a cantilevered roof to shade the grandstand and the box seats. If you will look beyond the show ring architecture and pay attention to the contest in the arena you will share in a centuries-old experience. The rider, horse and trainer have worked together for years to prepare for this moment in the show ring. Keep your eyes on the horses as they perform the commanded gaits, each one straining to be the best of the class. It is riveting and never fails to send chills of competitive excitement down the back of my neck.

Margaret Sue and I pack two ice chests, one for libation and general thirst abatement, the other for our supper and midnight snack. The idea is to be self- sufficient. Most of the rural counties in the Commonwealth are dry, which means that spirit beverages are not sold. I do not offer advice on the question of the appropriateness of packing a well-stocked bar to the horse show, but as in all things that are either important, profitable or fun, discretion has value.

When traveling to a Kentucky county fair horse show, you never know with whom you will spend the evening. We play it loose, choosing to see how the afternoon and evening will unfold. At times we will tailgate with other couples we encounter at the show. And at times we find friends and acquaintances, locate under an oak tree on the edge of the fair ground, making trips to the show ring. Everyone shares the contents of their respective ice chests, which lean heavily toward Country ham and rolls, cut fresh vegetables and dips, crackers and cheese. The lie is that we keep our supper light in deference to the heat. The truth is—fair food is close by.

In Kentucky that means grilled center-cut pork chop and grilled rib eye steak on a bun.

Only if pressed by the offer of a free box seat do I settle in one spot. The action is not in the seat, it is in the arena. At a county fair horse show, I am a railbird by inclination, that is for certain. I want to be close to the American Saddlebred horses in the show ring, looking them in the eye, feeling with them, their need to excel and to win.

Bird Hunting

Sometimes I think the entire year is a prelude to the Kentucky fall sporting season. It is not based on the Julian calendar, the orbit of the moon or the rotation of the earth. Fall begins for us on the first day of September every year and winter comes on Christmas day, drawing the fall sporting season to a close. Kentucky embraces the fall of the year and it is the best of times in Kentucky. No question about it, nothing compares with the sporting grandeur of Keeneland Race Course on any day in April or the week of the Kentucky Derby at Churchill Downs in May. But, if a favorite four-month part of the year is in the debate, the answer is—the fall.

I have had the honor of counting many farmers in central Kentucky as my friends. The permission that they grant me to hunt their fields in the fall of the year has been a lifetime of satisfaction. We are talking bird hunting here. The fast-flying mourning dove in September, the wary mallard duck in November and the cagey Canada goose in December are my quarry.

My association with hunting is exclusive to bird hunting. The magnificent game dinners that result from the hunt are warm convivial evenings, spent with childhood friends and comrades of the field. I find bird hunters to be a congenial lot, spending as much time grousing about the experiences shared in the autumnal fields and the frigid waters of our Kentucky rivers, streams, ponds and lakes as they do the actual shot. In character and by way of temperament my bird hunting companions have been and are, in an absolute sense, Kentucky gentlemen.

We like to sauté the doves in butter; or marinate them

overnight in orange juice and soy sauce, grill them outdoors with a sliver of hot pepper inserted into each breast and a half slice of bacon, secured with a wooden spear; or we will substitute the dove breast for beef in the Beef Masters recipe.

We filet the ducks, marinate them in butter and ground pepper and roast them on a very hot grill, medium rare.

The Canada is smoked, placing it on the cold side of the grill, covered and basting it with butter, continuously, 30 minutes to the pound.

Masters Steak Sauce and orange bourbon sauce are at the ready. Fine aged Kentucky bourbon whisky is in the glass.

The Fall Thoroughbred Meet

The fall racing season at Keeneland Race Course in October and Churchill Downs in November is a fabulous time for Margaret Sue and me. The hardwood trees turn golden, red and orange with the changing season. The bushes and shrubbery yield every color of crimson, yellow and brown. The migrating birds take to flight in great waves, responding to ancient instincts to find warmer climates and more abundant feeding grounds. The chill is in the air, as arctic air forces itself down into the rolling hills of central Kentucky.

Margaret Sue and I are creatures of the same autumn impulses, except our destination and change of venue is Keeneland and Churchill Downs for the fall race meet. We will go with a small group or hook up with our Lexington and Louisville friends at the track. Several trips will be to dine in their respective dining rooms, watching the racing panorama from the balcony of the club house, eating rare roast beef and sampling their stock of liqueurs. And several trips will be to join the crowd in the grandstand, bundled against the cold, supping on homemade burgoo purchased at the track and drinking hot coffee laced with a fine aged Kentucky bourbon whisky, poured from a flask, sequestered discreetly in the side vent of my coat. Perfect.

College Battle Cry

The college football season begins in Kentucky with the anticipation that this time, maybe, the boys on the gridirons across the Commonwealth will find a winning formula. Alas, over the past century our brave lads have all too frequently had to settle for the short end of the victory stick. Kentucky feeds on basketball and football has had a difficult ride. But dauntless in the face of adversity, the college football faithful load up their vehicles and usher in the fall tailgating season.

An excellent bar has been stocked in the trunk of the car. The Benedictine, pimento cheese, pecan chicken salad and bourbon cheese are secure in the ice chest. Chips, crackers, sourdough bread and the condiments are in the food locker. I am going to tell you, in all honesty, I love going to our college football games. There is a drama played out each week at our universities, full of hope and pathos. In spite of all of this, if Margaret Sue made me, I would be overjoyed to sit on a comfortable chair under a big fat tree on the college campus and listen to the game on the radio with a gang of fans in likewise sympathy. After all, the party is in the trunk.

Then, in a clash of resounding arms, and to the drum beat of war, basketball in Kentucky marches into the fall sporting season in December. In Kentucky, college basketball is a full body contact sport, and every Kentuckian from the cities to the "hollers" has a voracious appetite for victory on the hardwood. Winning is the only acceptable result, no excuses are tolerated and no quarter asked or given.

In this rancorous atmosphere the spontaneous battle cry is trumpeted to "come to the house and watch the game." And you may as well, the retail establishments are deserted, their owners and employees are listening to the game. Across the Commonwealth it is the same. I have known priests to take their radio and headset into the confessional box on Saturday afternoon so as not to miss the play of their team. I am certain the sinner across from him did, too.

In a Kentucky house there is only room for one team. Those for that team are in on the invitation. Those who are in opposition are excluded and that extends to marriages. This is serious business. McManus House is University of Kentucky, my neighbor is University of Louisville and they have never been to my house to watch the game, as there is no reason to set up an ugly situation. In Owensboro they are all about Kentucky Wesleyan, in Bowling Green it is Western Kentucky University, in Richmond it is Eastern Kentucky University and so forth.

Just as the season begins it breaks for the Christmas holiday, the battle to join the Final Four to be resumed after the new year.

"The Voice From Old Kentucky"

So you came back, after all, Colonel? When I saw you in Paris two years ago, you told me that Paris was your home. You said it fit you like an old glove; that the boulevards were made for you, and that you never expected to come over to this side of the pond again. How came you to change your mind?

"I got homesick."

"Homesick? Homesick? Well, that's good. Like a schoolgirl, eh? What do you think of that, gentlemen? The Colonel got homesick! He, who hasn't had a home for thirty years—who has been roaming the earth ever since Lee surrendered. Touch the button, Colonel, the drinks are on you."

"With pleasure, Judge, but pardon me if I fail to understand the cause of your merriment. As the doctor says, it has been many years since I have known a home; but—don't keep the boy waiting. A little bourbon for me. Yes, many years, gentlemen, many, many years. But, I was homesick, just the same. And I confess that the incident that sent me back will probably seem trivial and absurd to you. I had made my mind up to make Paris my home. For a wanderer like me it seemed like the proper haven. I like its ways. I like its playhouses. In fact, I like everything about Paris—except its taste in the manner of drinks. But you don't have to drink absinthe unless you care to, and I thought I was at last satisfied to settle down. I felt so thoroughly established that I began to think of doing some work, and actually did a little writing. This went on for a year or more, and I was fully determined to stay right there like an old hull on the beach, until the timbers fell apart.

"At last, some way or other, however, I began to feel a strong feeling of unrest. I got nervous. I began to worry about my liver. I consulted a doctor. He, the idiot, advised me to quit smoking, and I advised him to go to that place where people are supposed to smoke forever. I decided that I would run down to Rome and see the gay old town of dirty beggars and bid farewell to meat. It was just the time for the carnival, so to Rome I went. I didn't enjoy myself. I met many people I knew, but none for whom I cared. It's hard on a man to make merry all alone. I wondered who I had ever seen in the carnival before. I had a personal grievance against everyone who was enjoying himself. When some one threw a handful of confetti over me, I swore. I made up my mind to stay it out, however. I had a good window on the Corso, near the Piazza del Poplo, and there was no use running away. The blue devils would have followed me. You can imagine me sitting there all alone, biting a cigar, and frowning down upon the gay crowds in the Corso. Little girls pointed me out and threw confetti at me, and then, when I did not smile, said something about the evil eye and got away. The noise made my head ache. Some friends called out to me from passing carriages, and I almost forgot to return their salutations. But all of a sudden my ears caught a whiff of an old melody. At first, gentlemen, I was not sure. I thought the tune was just running through my mind. But someone was surely singing. I could catch the song and the tinkling of banjos away down the street. Very faint, but coming nearer:

"'Weep no Mo', my lady,
O weep no mo' to-day,
For I'll sing one song ob de old Kaintucky home,
Ob de old Kaintucky home far away.'"

"Doctor, I don't know what you would have made out of a study of my brain when I caught those words; but I knew that it darted electricity all through every nerve in my body. The singers were coming my way—four good, strong American boys (Woodford County boys, I'll bet). They were in an open carriage. When they got up under my window, I jumped up and gave a rebel yell that shook the Vatican. They looked up, laughed, and kept on singing. I strained my ears as they went down the Corso, and when I caught that last echo, hang it, gentlemen, there was a lump in my throat as big as your fist. I sailed for New York the very next week, and three weeks later I took a drink in Louisville."

"Well, here's to the boy. Everybody standing, please. Here's to 'The Old Kentucky Home!'" —**Anonymous**

"My Old Kentucky Home"

The sun shines bright in the old Kentucky home
'Tis summer, the people are gay;
The corn top's ripe and the meadow's in the bloom,
While the birds make music all the day;
The young folks roll on the little cabin floor,
All merry, all happy and bright,
By'n by hard times come a-knocking at the door,
Then my old Kentucky home, good night!

Weep no more, my lady,
Oh weep no more today!
We will sing one song for the old Kentucky home,
For the old Kentucky home far away.

— Stephen Collins Foster, 1853

Federal Hill (My Old Kentucky Home)

Stephen Foster wrote this song in 1853 after a visit he made to Federal Hill, the home of his cousins, the Rowen family of Bardstown, Kentucky. Federal Hill was purchased by the Commonwealth of Kentucky from the Rowen heirs in 1923 and is the state shrine that we call My Old Kentucky Home.

The song "My Old Kentucky Home," is the state song of Kentucky. There are two additional stanzas to the song but these are not traditionally sung.

We like to sing "one song for the old Kentucky home" prior to our sporting and official events, or whenever a sense of nostalgic majesty is required. When the song, "My Old Kentucky Home," is lifted to the heavens by the singing of it, I promise you, there is not a dry eye in the house.

Each summer the city of Bardstown hosts "Stephen Foster, The Musical". The great music composed by Stephen Foster is on revue and is a delightful evening, performed by a summer stock company of music and drama students from the colleges and universities in our Commonwealth.

The only peer of Stephen Foster as far as I am concerned is George Gershwin and I would lay down my bet at 3 to 1 that George was a student of Stephen's.

Elmwood

Elmwood

The master of Elmwood mansion, my father, known by all as Papa, delivered over ten thousand babies in the span of his medical career. Papa felt very grateful to his patients. He believed that he took care of them and that they took care of him. After he retired, when asked by former patients if he missed the practice of medicine he would proclaim that indeed he did – "the day before I retired, two thousand women adored me, the day after just one." This said with a twinkle in his eye and a peripheral glance in the direction of his wife, Mimi.

The old patriarch never really retired, he simply found other ways to engage his numerous friends and admirers. He grew a garden of four hundred and fifty rose bushes, selling the prolific production to them for fifty cents a stem, check made out to the medical school. Weddings and debutante balls could require as many as twenty-five dozen stems. No problem, he had it covered.

It would be a mistake to think of Mimi as only the supportive element in Papa's life or in the household life of Elmwood. Mimi had a mind and a career of her own. For many years she was an international buyer for a major department store in Kentucky, traveling to New York each month and to the European markets each year. The politically powerful and successful businessmen that were entertained at Elmwood found in her the Southern charm of a great lady and an intellect that challenged their own.

Mimi had an enormous influence on the lives she touched. She was a very accomplished hostess and entertained beautifully in the formal rooms of Elmwood. However, it was in her every day life that she proved most remarkable. Her evening meal was a five-star dinner; if she knew you were coming, she would set a place at the table for you. She invited the single, and the recently unmarried to Thanksgiving and Christmas dinner. At times the group was so large that the sixteen seat dining room table was insufficient and she hosted the dinner, buffet style. I can recount many times the dinner swelled to thirty or more. Those that were in on these dinners have commented on their memory of the event to us throughout their lives. Mimi did not want her friends or the friends of her brood to be alone on a festival day unless it was by personal choice.

The magic and allure of Elmwood in Louisville, Kentucky had a lot to do with the architecture and the age of the place. It was built in 1840 on a massive scale with fourteen foot ceilings and extraordinarily wide floor and ceiling moldings. Papa and Mimi had only two kinds of furnishings: old furniture, dated prior to Adams, "the first one" and furniture crafted by Papa, who was proud to be known as a cabinetmaker of consummate skill. A tour of Elmwood conducted by the master himself was an adventure not to be missed. But I am telling you that the powerful charm of Elmwood was not so much in its voluminous rooms as it was in the sofas and wing-back chairs filled with family and friends attracted to the mansion to be in the very excellent company of Papa and Mimi.

The bar at Elmwood was always open, a drink could be had

for breakfast, if one were so inclined. But I can not remember a time when the privilege was abused. The guests that came to Elmwood came to be with its stewards, to be embraced by an old style of Kentucky hospitality, chock full of simple courtesies and elegant manners.

Holloway House

Holloway House

There was a time in the early 1800s when a Kentucky farm was much more than the home place for a family. It was an economic center that produced nearly all of the means and materials a large and extended family group required to sustain its life and livelihood. Holloway House is an example of Kentucky life as it appeared in the emerging prosperity of the post-Revolution years.

Holloway House was constructed in 1820 by the architect John Rogers, who also built St. Joseph's Cathedral in Bardstown. The house is some 10,000 square feet, with a spiral staircase ascending to the third story ballroom. The plantation upon which it was built produced all of the brick and timber used in its construction. Most of the Holloway plantation out buildings are still extant, as they were constructed with the same three brick thick walls as the house. The smokehouse, icehouse and barns still stand next to the grand old mansion as sentinels to a time when the farm and plantation were the center of social and business life in Kentucky.

And it was here that Mama Sudie, Sue Carol's mother and Margaret Sue's grandmother, was queen of all that she surveyed. I did not have the pleasure of knowing E.T. Holloway, Mama Sudie's husband, but I wish I had known him. Mama Sudie was so fond of him. Every day living with Mama Sudie must have been an experience like no other. Mama Sudie treated life as her playground; she rarely missed a social opportunity. To her life was about seeing her friends. Whether they were rich or destitute, educated or illiterate, powerful or weak was not a judgment she felt the need to make. She invited them all to Holloway House to visit with her, and if they were sick or had passed away, she went to visit them. I saw her buy clothes at Saturday yard sales, clothes that she felt were attractive and sized correctly, to take to children she knew who were without pretty garments to wear to church or school. And with equal aplomb, she would entertain a Kentucky governor or senator or a host of dignified guests later in the evening.

Mama Sudie was married to E.T. Holloway for thirty-five years, living on and working a fifteen-hundred-acre plantation that had three dairies and extensive tobacco and timber acreage. Her sister-in-law, Margaret Holloway Veech, lived across the road on a seven-hundred-acre horse farm and also was married for thirty-five years. The two "sisters" lived the last thirty years of their lives with each other, their husbands having passed away. Every day Aunt Margaret would travel to the store to purchase the dinner for the evening, she being selected because Mama Sudie considered her the rich one, and every evening Mama Sudie would cook dinner for the two of them. On Sunday the Holloway family, the preacher, the recently engaged, and various friends and lost souls would gather in the great parlors of Holloway House, filled with early Kentucky cherry and walnut furniture and massive Victorian pieces, to share luncheon after church services.

The Sunday dinner, as it was termed, was a two-day enterprise at Holloway House, beginning on Saturday afternoon with Mama Sudie and Sue Carol baking cakes and vegetable casseroles. Early on Sunday morning, rolls, biscuits and breads were taken up, and left in their baking pans to rise, filling the great house with the aroma of yeast and freshly kneaded dough. The Sunday dinner crowd would arrive at half past twelve. The men would fill the chairs and sofas to talk the conversation of rural Kentucky: weather, crop health, livestock and market conditions. The boys and girls would play outside on the lawn or in the third floor ballroom if the weather was inclement. The women occupied themselves with the dinner, cooking the meal in both the summer and winter kitchens, the one being away from the house connected by a covered breezeway, the other inside the house. At three in the afternoon the table was set and a dining room table meant to seat eighteen would have twenty-five place settings of china plate, crystal glass, and silver from the various generations of the Holloway family.

On the sideboard was a tremendous array of foods, seemingly without a plan as to whether they complemented each other. The obligatory Country ham and fried chicken were there, as well as roast beef or turkey. Scalloped and mashed potatoes, broccoli casserole and corn pudding, baked oysters and stewed tomatoes, deviled eggs and banana croquettes were invariably present. A gallon of iced tea with four cups of sugar mixed in and coffee were the beverages. White cakes with creamy caramel icing were on hand as well as double-layered jam cakes, the centers filled with strawberry or blackberry preserves. The breads were on the table, to be passed throughout the meal.

Sue Carol, after an hour at the table, would then organize the scullery. She would summon each guest to his or her station. The roles of dish washing and hand drying were delegated to particular women, who had assumed their positions in the kitchen hierarchy decades in the past. The men would maneuver the furnishings back into their proper places. And then to complete their tour of duty, the men would act as couriers, carting the crystal and silver from the wash basins back to their home in the cupboards and on the shelves of the pantry. The entire work in progress was supervised relentlessly by Sue Carol, who required diligence from all of her help. The Sunday dinner contingency, after the chores were completed, would find the safe harbor of a favorite chair to spend the remainder of the day in pleasant discourse with those assembled.

I never tired of listening to Mama Sudie talk of the days when she and her mother would host similar dinners on the same kind of scale, without the benefit of running water or electricity. The heat for the ovens came from wood. The light for the rooms came from coal oil and candles. The water was hand pumped from the well. The meat came from the smoke-house and the poultry lot. And yet the same bountiful table was set and the dining table was packed with dinner guests.

Margaret Sue and I were married on the front porch of Holloway House, amidst the great columns, with a soloist above us on the second-floor balcony to help create the proper mood. The wedding guests were on the lawn in front of us. As the preacher invoked "Gawd's" great mercy and blessing, we felt very fortunate to have our love consecrated at Holloway House. Margaret Sue took my breath away, she looked so beautiful in her wedding gown. The fact that it rained toward the end of round one of the wedding ceremony, depriving the preacher of a full hour before us, did not dampen the happiness we felt on our wedding day. The folks on the lawn, all two hundred of them, simply packed into the parlors of Holloway House to sample the coconut and pineapple upside-down cakes prepared by Mama Sudie and Sue Carol. Gracious. It was an elegant affair. A second reception was held later in the evening at my club for those inclined toward strong drink, sumptuous food and very loud music.

McManus House

McManus House

Bardstown, Kentucky was occupied in the late 1770s by pioneer families who braved the hostile and dangerous conditions largely created by our nation's fight for independence from England. The American war with our English adversary and their Indian allies cost many a frontier life without regard to age or gender. Out of these desperate times, emerged a very hardy, tough and resilient Kentucky breed of men and women, intent on making Kentucky their home. Almost a thousand miles from civilized habitation, these Kentucky pioneers had to do for themselves.

It is amazing that under these harsh and hard circumstances a town as beautiful as Bardstown could be built at the turn of the 19th century, using the scarce tools and only the wood and stone available from the forest. The citizens of Bardstown built a magnificent cathedral, a hotel, large estate homes, a courthouse, schools for boys and girls, a college and a business marketplace by 1820. So many of our houses and stores have at least one log room and many of the houses, whether log, frame or brick, are supported in their floor, walls or roof with bark-on timbers, squared on the appropriate side with an adz.

The earliest houses, built prior to 1810, were constructed a room or two at a time with low ceilings and huge fireplaces. The most common way to accommodate the growing family was to construct the first room of log, thereby securing the family against the advancing winter. The next addition placed a frame or brick room against the existing log room and the following addition placed two rooms above those on the ground, creating a house plan of "two over two." If a level of affluence found favor with the owners of the property, an additional wing was added, usually another "two over two," giving the family, four rooms up and four rooms down. And by way of this description is the architectural history of our home, McManus House.

McManus House, residing within the historic district of Bardstown, was also built in stages, the log room having been constructed in 1797, with frame and brick additions in 1820 and 1840. The property was originally owned by my ancestor, Walter Beall, who developed Bardstown after the War of Revolution with England. Walter Beall sold the property to Charles McManus in 1796, who constructed our home.

McManus House has been the scene of so many fine times. It is not the imposing mansion of Elmwood or of the grandeur of Federal Hill, the My Old Kentucky Home state shrine. But it is almost as old as the Commonwealth itself and possesses a charm that is remarkable. Margaret Sue and I entertain inside the house in the wintertime, with the old fireplaces roaring with heat and good cheer. In the other three seasons, we are on the lawn using the great trees as our canopy. Margaret Sue and I have created a home that is warm and welcoming. We offer our neighbors, our family and our friends a very old and congenial atmosphere in which to enjoy life with us.

Margaret Sue and I see ourselves as the beneficiaries of a tradition of Kentucky hospitality that traces our family roots back to the original settlers in Kentucky and the original English families to land upon the American continent. When I am sitting in front of my garden at McManus House under the red bud tree on a hot, humid Kentucky summer day, I am satisfied. I am content that, although I am a modern man, I can still reach into my past for the solace that I belong to the family that first explored Kentucky and to a race of English people documented far beyond the Norman conquerors of that island. When I find myself in the soup of our Kentucky and English genealogy and share this history with my children, they rush to find other ways to occupy their time. This level of sentimentality is more than they can tolerate.

It is not by accident that we learn our hospitable way. Children, from the time they acquire language, are expected to rise to shake the hand of an adult entering the house, looking straight into their eyes, to show respect and to give a proper greeting. We address our children using "sir" and "miss" according to their gender from the day of their birth. The children respond in likewise fashion using "sir and "m'am." The cornerstone of our etiquette training is revealed in our language and is based in gratitude, using the words "please" and "thank you."

We include our children in our entertaining, teaching them the rules of courtesy and expecting them to make us proud with their polite behavior and respectful demeanor. We teach our children that they are the equal of anyone, regardless of their station or title and to treat all ranks in the social order with a polite countenance. In this way the doctor, lawyer and Indian chief as well as the hunting guide, bartender and carpenter are friends, each in their way. Once the social graces have been attended to, the party can begin.

Boonesboro

Boonesboro, Bryan Station and Waveland

In 1763 Daniel Boone left his family home in the Yadkin Valley of North Carolina to explore the lands west of the Appalachians. The British Crown had expressly forbidden the exploration of these lands, fearing the expansion of colonial influence so far away from British government and military control. The English army regulars stationed on the American continent had just concluded a protracted war with native Indians who were contesting colonial settlement of their homelands and annual migration routes on the frontier. Another war with France seemed to be on the horizon and a continuing conflict with Spain kept English military forces alert in Europe.

The Crown was beginning to feel the weight of the American colonies nascent expressions to separate from English rule. American dissatisfaction with English trade monopolies was appearing more ominous, the rhetoric on both sides of the

Atlantic Ocean becoming increasingly inflammatory as the English placed restrictions on American trading and settlement ambitions.

The opportunities to claim or have granted large tracts of land east of the mountains was diminishing, much of it having already been taken. Daniel Boone, restless and feeling enclosed, living amongst his neighbors in the Yadkin Valley, decided to explore the uncharted wilderness west of the mountains, declining to heed the admonishments of the Crown. An early explorer of Kentucky, John Finley, had found a pass through these mountains and had revealed to Daniel Boone his discovery of vast meadowlands with a gentle terrain of rolling hills and an abundance of streams and rivers. Boone spent the better part of the next ten years exploring, hunting and trapping the region we know as Kentucky.

Returning to the Yadkin Valley periodically, Boone interested a land speculator, one Richard Henderson, in financing an expedition to the Kentucky country. The idea was to survey the ground Boone had traveled, trading with Indians he had met, whom he thought would sell them the claim they felt they had on the land. The Henderson group would then petition the British Crown for a claim for millions of acres, and if denied, set up an autonomous government. The alternative plan, in the event of a separation from England, was to have the Commonwealth of Virginia, of which the Kentucky county was a part, to recognize and record the surveyed claim. The plan was to erect a series of fortified stations, to securely receive the settlers that would follow.

To this end, Boone gathered together men who shared his aspirations. Among these was William Bryan, who had married Boone's sister, Mary Boone. William Bryan and Mary Boone Bryan were my grandfather and grandmother of generations past. Daniel Boone then married William Bryan's niece, Rebecca Bryan, making Daniel Boone an ancestor by marriage and by blood.

Boone and Bryan along with thirty other men, made the journey through the wilderness to build Boonesboro, the first settlement in Kentucky in 1773. The following year the brothers-in-law, Boone and Bryan, along with other men, returned to the Yadkin Valley and brought their wives and children to Boonesboro. Bryan, several years in the Boonesboro fortification, struck out with several of his brothers to build Bryan's Station in 1776, about twenty miles west of Boonesboro, and about five miles from the fort at Lexington, built a year earlier.

In 1776 the Americans declared their independence from England, formed a government and set about the task of expelling the English from the North American continent. The English, determined not to lose the American colonies, used their army to attack the Eastern seaboard port cities, thereby severing the flow of supplies from Europe. The English strategy to attack the Americans west of the mountains was to launch the assaults from the English forts at Vincennes, Fort Sackville and Kaskaskia in the Illinois country, and to enlist the support of the Indians centered around Detroit and Chillicothe in the Ohio country. From these bases, Kentucky could be attacked by Britain, using English troops and their Indian allies. The stakes for the nations at war was immense, the control of the Northwest Territory east of the Mississippi River.

"A Visitor's Regret"

I must admit – although it hurts –
That I was born unlucky;
I've never, literally, had
A home in Old Kentucky.
And yet I feel, should wayward Chance
Direct my steps to roam there,
I'd meet you all and greet you all –
And find myself at home there!

– Dr. James Ball Naylor

The fighting was ferocious. My grandfather, William Bryan and his son by the same name, were killed in 1780 in the Battle of Bryan's Station in a savage attack by English and Indian forces led by the English commander Simon Girty. My grandmother, Mary Boone Bryan, was recognized for her heroism during the siege of Bryan's Station, when she left the fort to carry water from the spring, the guns of the British and

Waveland

Indians leveled upon her.

In 1783 the Americans signed a peace treaty with England, with the English ceding Kentucky and the Northwest Territory to the Americans. By their courage and sacrifice the pioneers of Kentucky had weathered the storm of war.

Boonesboro was my family's first home in Kentucky in 1773 and our family were among the first colonial inhabitants of Kentucky. Bryan's Station was our second home in 1776. Both had been cut out of the wilderness and defended with the lives of our family.

The son of William Bryan and Mary Boone Bryan, Daniel Boone Bryan, built Waveland plantation in Lexington after the Revolution with his heir, Joseph Bryan, completing the work in the middle 1800s. Waveland's two thousand acres was a self sufficient farming operation having a dairy, grist mill, distillery and a forge to support and process the agricultural production. Throughout the 19th century, Waveland was the center of horse racing and bloodstock breeding in Kentucky.

"Our Old Kentucky Home"

Finding comfort in the reflections of old Kentucky fosters an image of our state shrine, My Old Kentucky Home in Bardstown, Kentucky. For a Kentuckian this home represents his homecoming, the family gatherin', the political speaking or church revival followed by a picnic barbecue. The Home, as we call it, is our resting place. It is a home in our Southern past that allows us to exclaim, "Every Kentuckian has a home." And when we seek confidence and solace before going into battle, "We sing one song to My Old Kentucky Home."

At the first note of the "Marseillaise" the Frenchman straightens for the charge; amid the solemn cadences of "God Save the King," the Englishman bows to the accumulated reverence of centuries; at the swelling rhythm of the "Star Spangled Banner," the eyes grow misty in the recollections of a patriot's longing for the dawn, and we salute the flag that carries a nation's history and is resplendent with the glory of its hopes; "Yankee Doodle" stimulates and "Dixie" stirs to madness; but one song, "My Old Kentucky Home," alone has the power to soothe the restless pulse of care, and it comes like the benediction that follows after prayer. It voices a sentiment, it speaks a message, it stirs the deep wells of the heart as nothing else has the power to do.

—Richard W. Miller

Genealogy

I am convinced that the younger generation should not research their ancestral lineage. I take this attitude so I will not suffer under the illusion that my offspring will spend even a moment considering from whence they came. Youth is expended falling in love, competing for the winner's circle and recuperating from the effort of it all. Therefore, the joy in finding an interesting family-genealogy link pales in comparative significance. But to those of us who have passed the third pole in the four-pole race, it is an enjoyable pastime shared with many similarly-minded cousins and kin remotely related.

I do not, in any way, take anything that I find in genealogy as serious business. I like the Kentucky family ties and have an interest in the Maryland and Virginia family lines. Our family was among the first to enter those lands and I enjoy reading about those histories.

Our European royal ancestry has a certain fascination for me, but what I am to do with the information, I have not got a clue. I have decided that a royal ancestor is a mixed blessing. If you proclaim a royal connection there is a tendency toward disbelief. Those hearing the claim look for a mountain of money passed down from a royal treasury and, when the cash is not in evidence, scoff at the claim. No matter, the way I look at it, if those royal families had made it worth our time, we would still be "over there." And besides, the American stock is the blood I am proud to belong to.

However, Kentucky owes a great deal of our culture to England, Scotland and Ireland. When Daniel Boone and William Bryan cut the Wilderness Trail through the Kentucky forest to Boonesboro and Bryan's Station, they brought with them men, like themselves, who had been displaced for one reason or another in prior generations, from some of the great and wealthy families of Britain. These pioneers possessed a cultural heritage that had knowledge of and appreciation for grand architecture, distilled spirits and sound horseflesh.

Consequently, our early homes are Georgian in appearance, our bourbon whisky is based upon the Highland art and science of distilling and our horse-racing industry is the English and Irish model. In that we trumpet to the world that in Kentucky we are known for fine-aged bourbon whisky, fast horses and beautiful women should come as no surprise. Fate took the best of Europe and the known world and brought it to America, then we took the best of America and brought it to Kentucky.

Scotland

Alexander I King of Scotland 1078-1124 + Sybilla
David I The Saint King of Scotland 1084-1153 + Matilda
Malcolm IV King of Scotland 1141-1165
Fitzalan, Walter I Steward of Scotland d. 1177
William I King of Scotland 1143-1214 + Ermengarde
Alexander II King of Scotland 1198-1249 + Joan
Fitzalan, Walter II High Steward of Scotland d. 1230 + Angus
Alexander III King of Scotland 1241-1286 + Margaret Plantagenet
Stewart, James High Stewart of Scotland 1243-1309
Eriksdottir, Margaret Queen of Scotland 1282-1290
Balliol, John King of Scotland 1240-1313 + Isabel of Warren
Bruce, Robert I "the Bruce" 1274-1329 King of Scotland + Isabel
Marjorie Bruce + Sir Walter Stewart 1293-1327
Robert Stewart II 1314-1390 King of Scotland + Elizabeth Mure
Robert Stewart III 1340-1419 Regent of Scotland + Murietta Keith
Marjorie Stewart b. 1361 + Duncan Campbell Lord of Argyll b. 1453
Archibald Campbell 1446 -1513 Earl of Argyll + Elizabeth Stewart
Donald Campbell Abbot Lord Privy Seal + Margaret
Margaret Campbell 1571-1632 + Alexander I Magruder b. 1569
Alexander II Magruder 1610-1677 + Sarah Braithwaite b. 1638
Samuel Magruder 1660-1711 + Sarah Beall 1658-1743
Ninian Magruder 1686-1731 + Elizabeth Brewer b. 1690
Ann Magruder b. 1732 + Thomas Claggett 1713-1778
Ninian Claggett 1750-1805 + Euphon Wilson b. 1752
Mary Claggett 1787-1857 + Thomas W. Prather 1778-1857
John M. Prather 1808-1894 + Demarius Brink
Henry W. Masters 1824-1886 + Sarah E. Prather 1826-1892
William Irvine Masters 1856-1932 + Elizabeth Witt 1862-1932
Vernon Elser Masters 1893-1952 + Clara Alcorn 1898-1976
Vernon Edward Masters 1918-1996 + Barbara Gallagher b. 1926
Col. Michael Edward Masters b. 1949

England

William the Conqueror 1027-1087 + Matilda of Flanders
Henry I King of England 1088-1135 + Matilda of Scotland
Matilda 1102-1135 + Geoffrey Plantagenet V
Henry II Plantagenet King of England 1133-1189 + Eleanor
Richard I Plantagenet King of England 1189-1199
John Plantagenet King of England 1199-1216 + Isabella
Henry III Plantagenet King of England 1216-1272 + Eleanor
Edward I Plantagenet King of England 1272-1307 + Eleanor
Edward II Plantagenet King of England 1307-1327 + Isabelle
Edward III Plantagenet King of England 1327-1377 + Philippa
Thomas Plantagenet 1355-1396 + Eleanor de Bohun
Anne Plantagenet 1383-1438 + William Bouchier
John Bouchier 1412-1474 + Margery Berners
Humphrey Bouchier 1432-1471 + Elizabeth Tylney
Margaret Bouchier 1470-1551 + Thomas Bryan
Francis Bryan I of Ireland 1490-1551 + Joan FitzGerald
Francis Bryan II b. 1549 + Ann Smith
William Smith Bryan b. 1604 + Catherine Morgan
Francis Bryan III 1630-1677 + Sarah Brinker
Morgan Bryan 1671-1763 + Martha Strode
William Bryan 1733-1780 + Mary Boone
Mary Nancy Polly Bryan 1771-1818 + David Hampton
Cynthia Hampton 1798-1845 + Claiborne Cox
Mary B. Polly Cox 1819-1900 + Allen Witt 1816-1883
Elizabeth Witt 1862-1932 + William Irvine Masters 1856 + 1932
Vernon Elser Masters 1893-1952 + Clara Alcorn 1898-1976
Vernon Edward Masters 1918-1996 + Barbara Gallagher b. 1926
Col. Michael Edward Masters b. 1949

Entrées

I have dozens of recipes for beef, lamb, chicken, turkey, fish and pork and during the course of the year I find time to use a great many of them. My wife has always claimed that at heart I am a grill man, which is true. For family dining, I rarely cook our meat indoors; I cook on the grill in all seasons and all weathers.

But when we entertain, and our guests have traveled great distances to get to us, we want to fix those foods that they have come to remember us by.

The entrée is the centerpiece of our sideboard or buffet table. Depending on the climate and the number of guests in our home, we make a choice for the entrée. All of our recipes are easy to prepare but absolutely delicious. We cook plenty and present the entrée in as grand a fashion as we know how to do.

In our home, the silver serving pieces and our crockery do not live to dusty old age in the cabinets, They are brought out at every opportunity to give our entertaining a flair that tells our guests that they are special and important people in our lives.

I feel a great sense of satisfaction when I watch the women of our family hauling out the silver bowls, platters and chafing dishes. There is nary a piece that is similar as to style, size or era. Each piece has a history, each a previous owner or four—all of them known to us, all of them remembered.

1. Rare Beef Tenderloin

Rare beef tenderloin is always a special dinner. Although I find I cook beef tenderloin on special occasions, I acknowledge a preference for this cut of beef and serve it with little prompting. Cooked to perfection and presented on a silver tray the beef tenderloin is magnificent.

In our family we host our holiday dinners on the eve of the actual holiday. This allows our extended family to join us while reserving the holiday for their family and children. Beef tenderloin is our choice for the entrée. The more traditional fare will be served the following afternoon.

We like purchasing a young beef tenderloin that weighs in at about four pounds. When you purchase a beef tenderloin, ask the butcher to trim it for you. If you are in the dark as to what I mean, just let it lay, and take it on faith that the butcher is doing you a favor.

Marinate the beef tenderloin for a day prior to cooking. We like to use a marinade that consists of equal parts of red wine and olive oil. Rest the beef tenderloin in a glass-baking dish sized to accommodate the meat. Cover with plastic wrap and place in the refrigerator. Turn the beef tenderloin at least once.

The beef tenderloin I prepare depends on a high roasting temperature; 500 degrees is perfect. I coat the beef tenderloin with butter and place it on a roasting pan or on the cool side of the grill. You will cook the tenderloin for 10 minutes, turning once. You will then cook the beef tenderloin for another 8-10 minutes, depending on your oven or grill, resisting the powerful urge to turn it again. When the beef tenderloin has a hot-red center or is 135 degrees in the thickest part, it is done.

Three minutes prior to removal, cover the top of the tenderloin with blue cheese and return to the heat, allowing the blue cheese to soften. Grind black pepper generously across the top of the blue cheese.

Slice the tenderloin to a thickness of 1-inch on the diagonal. You will want to serve two or three slices to the plate. Drizzle Masters Steak Sauce sparingly over the tenderloin slices and leave a bowl on the side for those who desire more. I would allow about a half a pound of tenderloin per dinner guest, uncooked weight.

Accompany with yeast rolls, asparagus, new potatoes, stuffed eggplant and baked zucchini squash. Vanilla ice cream with chocolate sauce for dessert complete this very excellent dinner.

2. Beef Masters

A good Kentucky cook will have a version of this flavorful stroganoff dish. Do not be lulled into complacency by using inferior cuts of beef. I use strip steak, and would use beef tenderloin, nothing less. My dinner guests always come back to the buffet for a second pass. You will have more in the pan after your initial serving but they will return for more, I promise you. Beef Masters is evening fare and very dignified.

INGREDIENTS

4 oz. wild rice
1 # mushrooms, sliced
1 stick butter, cut in half
1 T fine aged Kentucky bourbon whisky
4-8 oz. strip steaks, fat removed, cut into 1-inch pieces
1 C red wine
2 beef-bouillon cubes, dissolved in 2 T hot water
2 T flour, dissolved in 2 T hot water
8 oz. sour cream
2-t seasoning salt
1-t pepper, ground

DIRECTIONS

✔ Cook the wild rice and set aside.

✔ Lightly sauté mushrooms in 1/2 stick of butter and set aside.

✔ Deglaze a skillet with fine aged Kentucky bourbon on a high heat. Add the remaining 1/2 stick of butter and the steak pieces.

✔ Sauté the steak until cooked to a light brown finish.

✔ Turn the heat down under the skillet to a low setting. Add the wine and the bouillon. Stir in the flour, holding back a little flour for additional thickening.

✔ Add the mushrooms and stir in the sour cream. It is important that the sour cream be added last, as sour cream breaks down quickly under heat. Stir in the seasoning salt and the pepper.

✔ Simmer for about 5 minutes; add the remaining flour, if necessary. Beef Masters is served thickened. Ladle Beef Masters over the wild rice. Accompany with a large Bibb lettuce salad. Serves eight.

3. Bourbon Glazed Filet of Beef

Your significant other will fall in love with you every time you prepare bourbon glazed filet of beef. Knowing this always inspires me to cook it on private evenings. I like to cook this dish for two but it expands nicely to four at dinner, if you can not find a way to keep company at bay.

If cooking for two, this is an easy dinner to cook while enjoying a fine aged Kentucky bourbon whisky and is further enhanced by a second drink of fine-aged Kentucky bourbon whisky while dining. After the dinner and dessert, send the guests home if you have them—for the evening has just begun!

INGREDIENTS
2 6-oz. filet of beef
1/2 C butter
4 oz. fine aged Kentucky bourbon whisky
pepper, ground

DIRECTIONS

✔ Sauté the filet of beef in the butter on a high heat until medium rare and place the beef tenderloin on the dinner plate.
✔ Deglaze the pan with a fine aged Kentucky bourbon and using a spoon make certain you capture the beef-butter
✔ Pour the glaze over the beef tenderloin. Grind black pepper onto the beef tenderloin and serve immediately.
Serves two. Double to serve four.

4. Buttered Lamb Chops

I have a longing for buttered lamb chops as for no other cut of meat. I enjoy a leg of lamb and have a fondness for mutton but I am passionate in regard to buttered lamb chops. They are perfection, straight out of the broiler or off of the grill. This fact mitigates against serving them in quantities appropriate for a huge gathering. I can manage about twenty at a time, which translates into serving them at a seated dinner for eight.

Although in the modern marketplace there does not appear to be a particular season of lamb availability, we seem to want buttered lamb chops in the cold of winter or the early spring. There is something about the warmth of the fireplaces at McManus House and the ambiance of our old home that seems to invite friends for a formal seated repast in our long narrow wood-paneled dining room.

A week prior to your need, order rib lamb chops from your butcher and ask him to delete the long bone; this will allow the lamb chops to better fit the plate. Ask the butcher to cut off any visible fat and to scrape the lamb chops. All of this is done easier by him than by us.

I rub the lamb chops with lemon juice and place them covered in the refrigerator for 2 hours. I then rub the lamb chops in garlic olive oil, seasoned with rosemary and basil.

Grill the lamb chops on a 400 degree grill or at a 3-inch height under the broiler. After searing well on both sides, move the chops to a cooler place on the grill or a 5-inch rack under the broiler. When the lamb chops appear cooked and the meat shows a pale pink in the center, the lamb chops are ready. The cooking will take about 25 minutes for 1-1/2-inch chops and about 15 minutes for 1-inch chops.

As you remove the lamb chops from the heat, spread softened butter across them. Grind black pepper and chives if you like onto the butter.

The buttered lamb chops vary in size and you will serve 2-3 to the plate, trying for even portions.

Accompany with wild rice, string beans, baked zucchini squash and a McManus House salad.

5. Trout with Lemon Butter

When I can, I serve trout. The small trout, white of meat and flaky when cooked, cannot be beat. We are blessed in Kentucky with more miles of streams and rivers than any state in the Union except Alaska. And many of these streams have trout.

Fresh from the stream trout are the berry patch. In the woods we savor trout on the grill, opened and rubbed inside and outside with olive oil and cooked over the coals. I am weak in the knees just thinking about the fine times we have spent, camping in the woods and catching trout for breakfast.

More often these days, I must admit, as my children have grown older and left home, I have lost my fishing buddies. Now, increasingly, I seek out fresh young trout in the fish markets. However, minus the nostalgia, the store-bought variety, if young and fresh, is delectable. I will recommend that you seek out the trout that is so young it has white flesh, not yet turned pink.

Regardless of the means by which trout comes to your kitchen, it is good and works well for a dinner of two or for eight. I have friends that remember their dinner of trout shared with us decades later.

If the trout still possess their heads and tails, cut them off. Or, if the task will distress the women folk, have the butcher do it before taking it to the house. The trout should already be split open; rub the trout inside and outside with lemon butter. Place lemon slices in row fashion along the length of the cavity; three slices should be sufficient. Broil or grill, at a 6-inch height the trout on one side, then the other, until the flesh is flaky and firm; guard against cooking the trout too dry.

Serve one trout per person, placing them on a platter in a row. Squeeze lemon across the top of the trout. Sprinkle slivered almonds, fresh parsley and chives for appearance and taste.

Accompany with wild rice, cold marinated asparagus, orange bourbon carrots and a Bibb lettuce salad. Lemon squares are for dessert.

6. Baby Back Ribs

Everyone gets really excited when the hue and cry goes up to cook baby back ribs. I only cook them occasionally but when I do, I tend to serve them for small groups of intimate family and friends, having never found a way to eat them or watch them being eaten without all concerned wearing the meal. I like to cook ribs on the hottest day of the summer and serve them in outdoor fashion on platters with chilled-red potato salad and corn on the cob. Serve this meal to your Yankee cousins and they will, God love 'em, never forget their visit.

There is hot debate on the proper method of cooking baby back ribs, but to my mind the real issue is to make the ribs fully cooked and tender, almost regardless of the cooking method. Cooking ribs is a suit yourself procedure.

A generation ago it was not uncommon for the host, or a hired man, to cook the ribs slowly over a smoking bed of hardwood coals for half a day, basting and turning them every ten minutes throughout the afternoon. The cooking of the baby back ribs was a warm weather rite, a ritual laced with rules and secrets. Alas, the romance found in an all-day cooking enterprise at home has gone with the wind for anyone past their college years.

As for choosing not to spend the day sweating over hardwood coals, do as we say in Kentucky, "don't think a thing about it." The taste and glory in baby back ribs is in the sauce. The Masters Steak Sauce I give you is simply great. Put a bowl of the sauce on the table. Your guests will love it.

There are probably as many ways to cook the baby back ribs as there are barbecue cooks. We use a dry rub procedure that is wonderful.

Concoct the dry-rub mixture. I will give you mine but I encourage you to add a little something extra, that you fancy—and keep it secret! In this way you will immortalize your barbecue as your own.

Mix a bowl of 2-t each of garlic powder, salt and Cajun seasoning. Rub it in on the top of the ribs. A very light amount of the dry rub is used, the idea being to season the ribs, not to coat them. Place the ribs covered in the refrigerator for two hours.

Place the ribs on a broiler pan. Preheat the oven to 500 degrees. When you put the ribs in the oven, lower the heat to 325 degrees. Bake the ribs for 1-1/2 hours. You do not need to turn them. If you grill the ribs outdoors, mound the charcoal on one side and place the ribs on the cool side of the grill.

After the ribs have cooked, coat the ribs on both sides with the Masters Steak Sauce and broil them at a 6-inch height, turning the ribs several times. Watch that you do not burn the sauce. If you finish the ribs over charcoal, place the ribs over the charcoal, turn them often. Either way, eventually, the ribs will form a nice crust and you will declare them ready. Supply all at table with damp cloth napkins.

7. Country Ham

I have found that my guests have a real taste and longing for Country ham, a ham-curing process revered by all who know it. The best hams have traditionally been those that have been aged between one and two years. These wonderful hams have graced our tables for over two hundred years.

That, having been said, let me tell you that there is little market demand for these great Country hams. The market is in that honey ham that we in Kentucky have always derided as city ham, dripping in a sugary mess, spiral sliced, the only age being the time it took to process it. I hate the way these honeyed hams look; I deplore the way they taste; I detest handling them, but to this generation they are sweet magnificence.

One of my friends, a researcher with a Kentucky university, performed a demonstration for us at a food trade show. He set out a platter of properly aged Country ham, a platter of honey-coated city ham and a platter of the caramelized pieces of the coating on the city ham, asking each of the thirty samplers of the platters which ham they preferred? Twenty-eight of the thirty chose the caramelized coating. My, my.

But if you want the real thing, the noble Country ham, then be bold and order it from your meat department if they stock it, or order from a dependable mail-order purveyor. It is almost certain that it will not have full aging but it will have some, three to six months being the modern standard. Ask for the cooked center slices, sliced thin.

I will give you the recipe for baking a whole Country ham, but most of you will not do it. Our generation is not fascinated with preparing a leg of anything.

8. Baked Country Ham

Buy a Country ham, optimally cured for at least one year. I will advise you to purchase a Kentucky Country ham, while disclosing my bias.

Soak the ham in water overnight. Next morning, wash ham thoroughly on both sides and scrub off any mold that you see. Trim off any hard surfaces on the cut side of the ham.

Fill a large roaster pan about half full of water. Put the ham into the roaster pan skin side down, initially, and cover. Place the ham in the oven at 450 degrees until the water begins to boil rapidly, then reduce the heat to 300 degrees. Cook 30 minutes to the pound and turn the ham every hour. After the proper cooking time has elapsed, turn the heat off and allow the ham to cool in the covered roaster pan for five hours.

Upon taking the ham out of the roaster pan, remove the skin and the fat layer, which will peel off easily. Drain the water from the roaster pan. Score the ham lightly in 1-inch squares and pat in cloves where the scored lines intersect. Then pat in cinnamon and black pepper. Put the ham back in the oven, uncovered and bake for 30 minutes at 400 degrees to brown the ham and seal in the seasonings. Allow to cool and refrigerate.

9. Chicken Breast Filet and Country Ham

Flatten a chicken breast filet. Place a layer of deveined cooked spinach onto the chicken breast filet along with a thin slice of Country ham. Fold the chicken breast filet over itself and secure with a wooden spear. Then bake until the chicken breast filet is done. Pour a few spoonfuls of melted blue cheese over the chicken breast filet prior to serving to complete a delightful, simple, elegant and flavorful dish.

10. Asparagus Wrapped in Country Ham

Cook asparagus. Then fold a thin slice of Country ham around 4-5 asparagus and secure with a wooden spear. Drizzle cheese sauce over each bundle and sprinkle with spring onion. Asparagus wrapped in Country ham, served with sliced beef and a Bibb lettuce salad, is a beautiful presentation.

11. Fruit and Country Ham

Place cantaloupe slices and red seedless grapes on a bed of Bibb lettuce, garnish with slivers of Country ham.

Cut the Country ham slice into medium size pieces and place the slices over a salad of grapefruit, orange and mandarin orange slices set upon a bed of Bibb lettuce. Drizzle French dressing on the top of the salad. Grind pepper over the salad.

12. Dressed Country Ham Sandwich

Cut a yeast roll or a soft egg roll in half. Spread both sides thinly with Hellmann's mayonnaise or smearcase. Cover one side of the roll with Bibb lettuce. Cut a peeled tomato thin and place on the bed of lettuce. Place 4 thin slices of Country ham and place them on top of the peeled tomato. Grind pepper onto the Country ham. Serve with red potato salad. It is the best dressed sandwich I know of.

13. Lemon Chicken and Country Ham

Take a chicken breast filet and flour it, knocking off all of the excess flour. Dip the floured chicken breasts in beaten egg, then dredge it in finely rolled breadcrumbs. Sauté the chicken breast in a small amount of olive oil until done. Squeeze a quarter of fresh lemon onto the chicken breast. Place a thin slice of peeled tomato on top of the chicken breast and sprinkle with basil. Add 3 thin slices of Country ham. Sprinkle blue cheese lightly across the top.

14. Country Ham Breakfast

Country ham served skillet hot with scrambled eggs, baked cheese grits, a chilled peeled tomato; a bowl of cantaloupe and breakfast biscuits is a classic.

15. Pork Tenderloin

Pork tenderloin has virtually no fat and really no moisture. It is a smallish cut of pork; a 1-1/2 pound tenderloin serving about four. I find that we cook pork tenderloin in the winter months but the reason escapes me.

The preparation of our pork tenderloin may seem off center; I make that remark each time I cook it. That said, it is fabulous. My cousin, who manages a big resort hotel, was satisfied it was the best pork tenderloin he had ever eaten and directed his staff to adopt it. Or so he told me.

Make a sauce of 1/2 C strawberry jam, 2 T white wine, 2-t fine minced garlic and 1-t black pepper.

Spread a coating of the sauce generously across the top of the pork tenderloin. Place a long piece of tin foil on the counter and with a knife cut three 1-inch slits at various places in the middle portion of the tin foil to allow the liquid to drain.

Place the pork tenderloin on the tin foil, wrap it tight and place it on a broiler pan. Bake at 350 degrees for one hour, open it, make certain no pink is in evidence; grind black pepper on top and broil for about five minutes to give it a good color.

Slice the pork tenderloin in 2-inch cuts.

Accompany with twice-baked potato, broccoli and cauliflower with lemon-butter and a spinach salad.

A pork tenderloin will serve about four.

"Kentucky—A Toast"

Kentucky – not the oldest nor yet the youngest; not the richest nor yet the poorest; nor the largest nor yet the least; but take it all in all, for men and women, for flocks and herds, for field and skies, for happy homes and loving hearts, the best place outside of heaven the good Lord ever made.

– Rev. Hugh McLellan,
in The Louisville Times

16. Burgoo

In the Kentucky heart dwells a place for burgoo. It is neither a soup, nor a stew, nor an entrée. It is so good that when we plan a day at Churchill Downs or Keeneland Race Course our interest in finding the burgoo competes with our desire to play the horses. The magnificence of burgoo is appreciated best in the out doors, with the wind in your hair. A glance at the recipe for burgoo is intimidating at first glance. Nonetheless, look it over several times and you will note that it is harmless, a wedding between fresh meat and vegetables. The trick to making a good burgoo is to add the vegetables in the second half of the cooking endeavor.

I have read many burgoo recipes, some dating back one hundred years and more. I am certain that in our frontier past many an elk, buffalo, and wild boar found a place in the burgoo. Burgoo is an ever-changing landscape. This recipe is a late 20th century version, a time when domesticated meats have been available; therefore, you will have no trouble recognizing the ingredients.

Accompany with a fine aged Kentucky bourbon whisky for your drink. Burgoo and bourbon have always been the best of friends. If you find that your facilities require that you cook the burgoo in your kitchen, take it outside to serve and eat. The spring and fall seasons work well for the presentation of burgoo for it is a sporting dish that feeds the hunter and the returning warrior!

INGREDIENTS

1 C olive oil
4 onions, diced
3 # beef shoulder, shredded
2 # pork tenderloin, cubed
4 # chicken breast, filets, cubed
3 gallons water
1 gallon chicken stock, can
1 gallon tomatoes, can, diced
5 carrots, diced
2 head cabbage
10 ears of corn, scraped off of cob, corn milk scraped off
1 T salt
Tabasco Sauce to taste

DIRECTIONS

✔ Use a five gallon stock pot. On a medium heat brown the onion then the meats. Never allow the burgoo to boil. After browning the meats, just simmer.

✔ Add the chicken stock and water and allow the burgoo meat to simmer for 1-1/2 hours, stirring every 10 minutes.

✔ Debone and shred the meat.

✔ Add the vegetables and simmer in the burgoo for 1 hour. Ten minutes prior to serving, add the salt and the Tabasco Sauce. The burgoo should be served thickened. Serves 25

17. Chicken Breast Filet in White Sauce

I have a circle of friends that I cook for. I guess that is the way to say it. Their children are grown and have left the nest. At some point during the month the prospect of cooking another intimate dinner for two begins to gnaw at them. They call me with an offer to bring over chicken breasts, with a request that I cook chicken breast filets in white sauce.

I know that they are capable of cooking the dish but then it would be a night in instead of out for them. Out of meanness I always allow them the task of scullery after dinner, while I take my ease and keep them company. To date they have not shown any signs of rebellion.

INGREDIENTS

4 boneless chicken breasts, flattened.
2 T olive oil
salt
pepper
2 T butter
1/2 C Half and Half
1/4 C flour
1 lime, skin grated, then juiced
1/2-t chives, dried
1/2-t dill, dried
salt and ground pepper

DIRECTIONS

✔ Flatten the chicken filets. Sauté the chicken filets in the olive oil until done. Season with salt and pepper and set aside.

✔ In a separate sauté pan, stir in the butter and Half and Half over a medium heat. Add in the flour slowly, and stir with a whisk, until all is thickened.

✔ Stir in the grated skin and juice of the lime, chives and dill.

✔ Allow the sauce to settle down for 5 minutes over a very gentle heat before serving.

✔ Season with salt and pepper to taste.

✔ Place chicken filets on a platter and swirl the white sauce around on top.

18. Turkey Hash

INGREDIENTS

1 onion, chopped
1/4 C butter
4 C chicken stock
3 T flour
4 C turkey breast, boiled cooked and diced
2 C potatoes, cooked and diced
salt
pepper

DIRECTIONS

✔ Sauté the onions in the butter until translucent. Transfer the contents of the sauté pan to a larger pan.
✔ Add the remaining ingredients. Stir until thickened.
Serves eight.

19. Creamed Chicken Louisville

INGREDIENTS

1 C chicken broth
1 # mushrooms, sliced
1 green pepper, diced
2 T butter
1/2 C flour
1 C Half and Half
1 T white wine
4 C chicken breast, boiled cooked, cubed
1/2-t salt
1/2-t pepper
1/2-t paprika

DIRECTIONS

✔ In a large pan, pour in the chicken broth. Simmer mushrooms and green pepper until just soft.
✔ Add butter and flour, whisk until well dissolved.
✔ To a very low heat, add the Half and Half and the wine.
✔ Add the remaining ingredients. Stir until thickened.
Serves eight.

Vegetables

My way of presenting a luncheon or dinner is to serve the entrée, a vegetable or two, a salad, bread and a dessert. I make certain that I have plenty. Whatever is left over is Sunday lunch!

In a former day, this notion of plenty was greatly expanded. There would be two or three meats, heaping bowls of soufflés and casseroles, every manner of cooked vegetables, compotes of fruit and numerous salads, breads and desserts.

In these modern times, we find ourselves more moderate, finding longevity a virtue. The vegetables I present to you are recipes I use throughout the year. I have always fled from casserole and I run smartly away from soufflé. But I find myself drawn to certain vegetable recipes that I can prepare quickly, have a good appearance and that my guests are wild about.

20. Bourbon Sweet Potatoes

Sweet potatoes, they are an odd potato, queer to look at and unseemly to handle. However, let me tell you in all honesty, you will rarely cook a vegetable this good. I have sampled dozens of recipes from every corner of the South and I consider this recipe for bourbon sweet potatoes the standard by which all other sweet potato dishes must rise to meet. In simpler words, bourbon sweet potatoes are excellent.

For many years, I did not prepare bourbon sweet potatoes, deferring to Mimi of Elmwood, who always volunteered to bring them to our larger social functions and sent them home with us when we visited with her—admonishing us, invariably, to return the bowl. I have always adopted, shamelessly I admit, the good recipes perfected by Mimi at the Elmwood mansion. Bourbon sweet potatoes is her recipe, as far as she knows and as far as any of the rest of us care to know.

For those who partake of bourbon sweet potatoes for the first time you will notice some alacrity, as they place a speck upon their plate out of courtesy to their host. You can tell by their comments, that for them the sweet potato is an anomaly of

Southern cuisine, certainly to be tasted but not to be over-enjoyed. After sampling, however, they return for a more substantial helping with exclamations of delight. This recipe travels well; like Mimi, we have sent it home with our guests on innumerable occasions.

INGREDIENTS

6 sweet potato, boiled until fork tender and peeled
1/2 C fine aged Kentucky bourbon whisky
2 eggs, beaten
1/2 C pecans, chopped
1/2 C sugar
2 T butter
1/4-t cinnamon
1/4-t nutmeg

DIRECTIONS

4 Mix all of the ingredients at a medium speed until smooth. Pour all of the ingredients into a well oiled baking dish.
4 Bake, lightly covered at 350 degrees for 45 minutes.

21. Asparagus

The queen of vegetables is asparagus. When we can find the long slender, young asparagus we serve it at the next meal. At Elmwood, Mimi peels the asparagus with a paring knife, a practice that makes eating the asparagus a transcendental experience. As much as I love peeled asparagus, I don't peel 'em; I don't have the patience for it but have mercy on me, it is good.

The meal period does not dictate our use of asparagus, just the availability of the younger stalks.

The best way to store asparagus, if purchased for cooking a day or two later, is to clip the base about 1/2-inch, and stand it tips upright in a glass or measuring bowl, anything with high sides, fill the container with water and refrigerate. You will be pleased with the result.

When time for cooking, remove the asparagus from the refrigerator and cut or snap off the bottom third of the asparagus stalk. You are trying to sever the hard part of the stalk from the tender part, which you will cook.

22. To Cook Asparagus:

Steam or boil in water that just covers the stalks for about 10 minutes. The asparagus is ready when the base is just this side of fork tender.

23. Asparagus and Country Ham

It is worth mentioning asparagus and Country ham a second time. Cook the asparagus. Wrap 4-5 asparagus in Country ham, secure with a wooden spear and pour a drizzling amount of cheese sauce over them. If you feel the need to do more of something, sprinkle chopped fresh spring onion on top after placing in a serving dish. A bit of spring onion works with almost everything.

24. Asparagus and Cheese Sauce, Sour Cream Dressing or Lemon Butter

Cook the asparagus. Place the asparagus in a serving bowl and drizzle cheese sauce, sour cream dressing or lemon butter over them. Grind pepper on top.

25. Cold Marinated Asparagus

Cook the asparagus. Marinate in vinaigrette with pimentos as a garnish and refrigerate for two hours prior to serving. We enjoy cold marinated asparagus for breakfast, lunch and dinner.

26. Orange Bourbon Carrots

A cooked carrot has always been tough for me. I find myself wanting to do more with it than simply putting carrots to a boil. The solution is orange bourbon sauce. We have always found a way to cook with bourbon, enjoying its ability to impart its own magnificent flavor while also bringing out the flavor of the food it is paired with.

Carrots glazed with orange bourbon sauce resolve my cooked carrot problem. I love to serve orange bourbon carrots and my guests love to eat them. The cooked carrot is rarely a standout but orange bourbon sauce transforms this bland tuber into a dish that prompts requests for the recipe.

After scraping the carrot, cut into marble size pieces. Boil in salted water for about 10 minutes, no more. Drain the carrots, place in a baking dish with about 1/4-inch of water, drizzle orange bourbon sauce over the carrots, cover and bake at 325 degrees for 30 minutes. Delightful.

27. Broiled Browned Potatoes

You will be astounded at the good taste of broiled browned potatoes. In our quest to divorce our cooking from the heavy oils of the deep fryer and the skillet we have migrated to the broiler to achieve even better results. All at table will heap praise upon this very simple hash brown.

In McManus House these potatoes are as popular for dinner with grilled T-bone as they are at breakfast with Country ham and eggs. You will love the way they puff up.

INGREDIENTS
4 Idaho potatoes, skinned
1 T butter
2-t seasoning salt
2-t garlic powder
pepper, ground

DIRECTIONS

✔ Cut the potatoes lengthwise into 1-inch wide slices.

✔ Boil the potato slices until fork tender, and then drain in a colander. When dry, drizzle on the butter, sprinkle on the seasoning salt, garlic powder and grind pepper onto the potatoes.

✔ Tumble the potatoes in the colander until all of the potato slices are coated.

✔ Place the potatoes in a single layer on a baking sheet that has been sprayed with cooking oil, and broil until brown, turning one or two times until all of the potato slices are golden. Serves six.

28. Stuffed Eggplant

Stuffed eggplant has been served in Kentucky for many generations. It has been a signature dish at many of the great hotels and inns. It is a very elegant dish that is easy to prepare and offers an outstanding presentation. We serve stuffed eggplant in all seasons, though we like it best served in wintertime formal dining.

INGREDIENTS
1 large eggplant
1-1/2 C water
1 C onion, chopped
1 T butter
1 T parsley, chopped
1 can cream of mushroom soup, undiluted
1 C mushrooms, sliced thin
1-t Worcestershire Sauce
1 C Ritz cracker crumbs (24 crackers)
1/2-t salt
1-1/2 C water
1 T butter, melted

DIRECTIONS

✔ Slice around the top of eggplant, leaving a bowl of the eggplant. Scoop out the eggplant flesh to within 1/2-inch of skin, taking care not to tear skin. In a pan simmer the eggplant flesh in the 1-1/2 C of water, about 10 minutes, and when done, drain thoroughly and set aside.

✔ Sauté the onion in the butter until clear and set aside.

✔ Then in a large bowl, combine eggplant flesh, parsley, mushroom soup, mushrooms and Worcestershire Sauce, salt and all but 3 T of the crackers and mix gently with a wooden spoon.

✔ Pour 1-1/2 C of water into a baking dish. Place the eggplant into the baking dish, making certain they do not lopsize. Drizzle the melted butter on the top of the eggplant and top with the remaining crackers.

✔ Cover and bake at 375 degrees for 1 hour.

Serves six.

29. Peeled Tomatoes

When I serve tomatoes, I serve them peeled. My nutrition obsessed friends berate me, for it seems to them that I have violated some code of conduct, but believe me when I tell you that they, and all others at table, rave about my peeled tomatoes. I serve them in several different ways, according to my mood. I only peel locally-grown vine-ripened tomatoes. I may cook with tomatoes that are not vine-ripened in the wintertime, but I do not like them, never have and never will!

30. Peeling and Serving A Tomato:

You will need to have a pan of boiling water and a bowl of ice water ready. Boil the tomato for 10 seconds. Recover the tomato with a slotted spoon and place into the bowl of ice water, for about a minute. The tomato skin can now be removed easily with a small paring knife. Refrigerate for use within the hour.

Breakfast

Cut thick and sprinkle with chopped basil, ground pepper and a pinch of salt.

Luncheon

Sliced medium onto a bed of Bibb lettuce with pecan chicken salad centered in the tomatoes. Garnish around the outside of the plate, with the fresh fruit of the season. My favorite fruits are blueberry, strawberry, cantaloupe and honeydew.

Dinner

Sliced about 1-inch thick and placed on a bed of Bibb lettuce on a salad plate. Top with a generous spoonful of smearcase. Garnish with chives and ground pepper.

Snack

Cut two pieces of fresh bread and spread smearcase or Hellmann's mayonnaise on each slice. Place 3 slices of tomato and 3 slices of crisp bacon. Salt and pepper to taste.

31. Baked Cheese Grits

Grits. Nobody ever seems to know what to do with 'em. To the uninitiated, espying them in a bowl or on a plate, only intensifies the mystery. To resolve the matter, most encounters with grits are resolved by not eating them and then reporting that, "I just don't like 'em." Not to be obstreperous—but grits are great. I know the odds are against me gaining converts to grits. I love 'em but I have grown up with 'em morning, noon and night.

But as for grits, they are at their best as baked cheese grits. I wish I could tell you I use regular grits, cooking them for an hour, then preparing the recipe. Regular grits taste better. However, I use quick grits, heresy to those who were my teachers.

And yet my Yankee friends are crazy about this dish; they feel very Kentucky when they eat it. They proclaim the mystery of grits upon viewing them, but they are soon relieved to smell and taste ingredients familiar to them. It is one of those foods guests tend to remember you by. So many times I have heard our guests from the northern regions exclaim, years later, how impressed they were with our hospitality and their experience with—grits!

INGREDIENTS

2 C quick grits, cooked
2 C sharp cheddar cheese, grated
1 C Half and Half
1/2 C butter, melted
1 T garlic powder
1-t salt
1/2-t pepper
4 egg yolks, beaten
1/2 T parsley, chopped fine
6 spring onions chopped fine

DIRECTIONS

✔ Cook the grits according to the instructions.

✔ Add in the remaining ingredients, except the parsley and the spring onions, stirring briskly with a whisk. Pour the grits into a well oiled baking dish.

✔ Bake at 360 degrees for 30 minutes.

✔ Then garnish the top with the parsley and spring onion. Serves six-eight.

32. Twice-Baked Potato

Serve this potato whenever you have grilled meat. It is special. If you find it convenient, the potato mixture can be made up the morning of. Allow it to cool, then cover and refrigerate. Add 10 minutes to the baking time if refrigerated prior to heating.

INGREDIENTS
4 potatoes, large and baked
olive oil
1/2 C onion, finely chopped
2 T butter
1 C sharp cheddar cheese, grated
1 C sour cream
1-t salt
1/2-t pepper

DIRECTIONS

✔ Wash and dry the potatoes, then coat the skins with vegetable oil. Pierce each potato 4 times with a fork to allow steam to escape. Bake the potatoes at 375 degrees for about an hour or until a fork slides into them easily.

✔ Cut each potato in half, lengthwise. Pick up each potato half with a toweled hand and scoop out potato flesh, leaving a potato shell. Be careful not to tear the potato shell.

✔ Sauté the onion in the butter until soft and set aside.

✔ Place potato flesh into a mixing bowl. Add the onion, sour cream and season with the salt and pepper. Add the cheddar cheese but with 2 T of cheddar cheese held back. Mix at slow speed until the potato flesh is smooth.

✔ Place the potato shells into a baking dish. Then, using a spoon, place potato flesh back into their shells, until big and heaping, being careful not to let them lopsize.

✔ Sprinkle the potato tops with the held back cheddar cheese.

✔ Bake at 350 degrees for 15 minutes, then broil the top until the cheese is brown.

33. Elegant Mashed Potatoes

This mashed potato dish is so good I find I must make a larger quantity than the usual allotment of one potato per guest. The key to great mashed potatoes is in the tasting of them after you add the ingredients. When they taste right, they are ready to serve.

Peel 8 medium size Idaho potatoes and quarter them. Place them in boiling water and cook them until they are fork tender. When they are tender enough, place the potatoes in a colander and allow them to drain.

Place the potatoes in a mixing bowl and mix them on slow speed until they are of a coarse consistency, then mix on medium speed for half a minute.

Return the mixer to slow speed and put in 1 C of sour cream and 4 T of butter. When thoroughly blended, add 1 T of green onion chives and 1 T of salt.

At this point you must taste the mashed potatoes for correct seasoning. Add salt if your taste requires more. If the desire strikes to add additional sour cream, resist it.

Place the mashed potatoes in an oven-proof serving dish and sprinkle the top with chopped spring onion. Sprinkle with paprika, lightly. Cover the serving dish tightly and place in a 275-degree oven until ready to serve. The mashed potatoes will dry out quickly and therefore I try to serve them within 20 minutes. Serves six and doubles easily.

34. New Potatoes

When I am serving rare beef tenderloin, new potatoes are present. I have a decided preference for the smaller new potato and find myself judiciously culling through the new potato selection to find them. I have really not decided that these smaller new potatoes have superior taste qualities but they present a fine appearance on the plate.

Collect four new potatoes per guest. Simply pare a strip around the potato about 1-inch wide, while lifting out any unseemly potato blemishes. Place them in a boiling pan of water and cook them until fork tender. It is essential that the new potatoes are not over cooked.

Drain the new potatoes in a colander. Pour enough melted butter on the new potatoes to give them all good coverage. Sprinkle fresh chopped parsley generously upon the new potatoes. Add salt to taste and add paprika for color. Toss the new potatoes gently, so as not to break them and add more parsley and paprika. Serve immediately.

35. Broiled Zucchini Squash

Zucchini squash is good almost anyway you fix it. My crowd always bellows for this recipe. The appearance of this squash, sliced lengthwise next to a beef rib eye is electric. It is as if nobody ever thought of doing it this way. Of coarse, it did not originate with me; it is the way we have always done it.

Serve 2 halves to a plate. Make as many as you have guests.

INGREDIENTS
4 small zucchini squash
1 T butter, melted
1/2 C slivered almonds
1-t salt
1-t pepper
paprika
lemon

DIRECTIONS

✔ Slice the ends off of the squash, and then slice in half, lengthwise. Place the squash upright in a baking dish, taking care they do not lopsize.

✔ Cut a shallow slice down the middle of each squash. Drizzle the butter across the top of the squash and season with salt and pepper.

✔ Broil until brown and fork tender.

✔ Place on a serving dish. Sprinkle the slivered almonds, then add the paprika for color. Squeeze some fresh lemon across the top if you have a fancy to, lemon is good on almost everything.

36. Green Beans, Central Kentucky Style

I know green beans. Like squash and tomatoes, green beans are a staple in the Kentucky garden. I guess if there is a cooking procedure, we do it for green beans. We pickle, sauté, boil, bake, poach, blanche and stir-fry green beans.

But my favorite is the simply boiled, wonderful taste of green beans. Buy them young, long and slender and by all means, buy a stringless variety. I cannot stand stringing green beans, though the elder members of my family find my distaste for stringing green beans indolent. Begging your pardon, I am just not going to do it.

INGREDIENTS
2 # green beans
3 T olive oil
2-t Tabasco Sauce
1/2 T seasoning salt
1/4 C almonds, slivered
1 lemon, fresh squeezed

DIRECTIONS

✔ 4 Clip the ends off of the string-less green beans.

✔ Place in pan of boiling water to cover. Pour the olive oil, Tabasco Sauce and seasoning salt on top of the green beans. Turn the beans over one time. Do not stir the green beans again. This is very important. Reduce heat to a simmer, just a bare bubble and cover with a tight fitting lid.

✔ Cook for 40 minutes, never stirring, as stirring will break the olive oil glaze on the green beans.

✔ Drain, add the slivered almonds, a squeeze of lemon, pepper, toss gently and serve.

Serves six-eight.

37. Broccoli and Cauliflower

Things always appear right with the world when we see florets of broccoli and cauliflower in a bowl, steaming at the end of the sideboard. We like to have them share the same bowl, feeling good about their combined presence.

We like to steam the florets of broccoli and cauliflower, briefly, just to the point of fork tender, then, flavored with the cheese sauce, sour cream dressing or lemon butter. Carefully, drizzle one of the sauces over the broccoli and cauliflower. The idea is to enhance the flavor of these vegetables, not to saturate. Grind pepper over the florets. Wow!

In the summertime we like to add zucchini and yellow squash. We sauté the vegetables separately as they soften quickly. We prefer our vegetables fork tender not mushy.

38. Wild Rice

I cannot imagine a better tasting food than wild rice. The nut-like flavor seems to complement every entrée. The tendency to mix wild rice with either white or brown rice is unfortunate. The fine taste of wild rice stands on its own. I often serve wild rice instead of a potato.

39. Baked Onion

The onion—chopped, diced, sliced and ground—rarely gets an opportunity to share center stage with other vegetables as a main coarse. As acrid and pungent as a raw onion is, baked, the onion is sweet and mild.

You will use medium white onions on the small size. Cut off the ends of the onion so that it will stand up on end. Strip the onion of the outer skin and the first layer. Cut a couple of shallow slices in the top of the onion, careful not to pierce the outside layer. Rub the entire onion with a light coating of butter, and press some of the butter into the slices you made in one of the ends.

Wrap each onion in tin foil and place in a baking dish, standing upright, so that the butter you forced into the end slices will work itself down.

Bake at 350 degrees for 1 hour.

Remove tin foil; place in a serving bowl, squeeze fresh lemon onto the onions and garnish with paprika. Grind pepper to taste. Provide one onion to each plate.

Pick Up Foods

Informal dining in Kentucky only means that to sit or not to sit is by the choice of the guest and that the meal to be shared will be casual. We have often presented an entire dinner or luncheon at McManus House requiring only wooden spears as the eating utensil. The idea for this kind of service is to allow the guests to eat, drink and socialize either standing or seated, without having to carve an item on their plate.

In the heat and humidity of a hot Kentucky summer, we often present a bountiful table of pick up foods. This kind of food presentation also works well for social occasions where people come and go, as at Christmas or prior to an event.

The pick up food idea is, additionally, useful when you find yourself having to throw something together quickly for an occasion that will not fit into your dining room and you are completely in the dark as to the number of people that will descend upon your property. We threw a party for the daughter of our dear friends a few years back, announced only a week earlier, the wedding ceremony was to be performed later in the month. The invitations went out by passing the word, pigeon and telephone. It appeared that time was of the essence. We received compliments on our table for years and we were far from gussied up.

The social occasion may be casual and the dinner informal but the foods presented will be from outstanding recipes, honored by time. The table so prepared usually has ten to fifteen food choices, inviting the guest to place upon their plate as little or as much as they wish. I present the pick up recipes I seem to gravitate toward and that I find are respected and appreciated throughout Kentucky.

You will find that Benedictine and pimento cheese, if used on an informal buffet table, are usually spread on white sandwich bread and then diagonally quartered. You will need to cover the plate of sandwiches with plastic wrap until served as the bread so quartered dries out quickly; however, if used as an appetizer, then crackers are provided.

40. Pimento Cheese

When you prepare pimento cheese you will be amazed to find the many ways in which your guests choose to use it. Those who are familiar with this spread will use it as contemplated, but will also combine it with other finger sandwiches leaving one of the bread tops an orphan. The clandestine operation I often see executed is the Benedictine-pimento cheese combination, performed as often as not with an accomplice, who watches your back, knowing you will return the favor. Margaret Sue has always growled at me for the practice, although I find her accepting of others who engage in it.

I have often seen pimento cheese heaped onto a winter's afternoon chili and have seen it added to a club sandwich, all surreptitiously taken from the confines of the bowl in which it resides.

INGREDIENTS

1/2 lb. sharp cheddar cheese, shredded
1/2 lb. mild cheddar cheese, shredded
1/2 C Hellmann's mayonnaise
1/4 C pimentos, diced
1-t pepper, cayenne
sugar, pinch

DIRECTIONS

✔ Add in all ingredients at slow speed in a mixer at very slow speed until all ingredients are blended but cheese is still of a coarse texture.

✔ Place in a covered container and place in refrigerator overnight to blend the flavors.

Serves 12, if served with crackers. Serves 10, if spread on thin bread, then quartered diagonally. Serves 6, if they are layering in onto whole slices of sandwich bread. Serves 1, if you spy someone attacking it with a spoon standing in front of the refrigerator door.

41. Benedictine

In the Bluegrass Region of Kentucky we have enjoyed Benedictine throughout the 20th century. Created by a restaurateur of that name, it has graced the finest Kentucky tables. It is served either as an appetizer on crackers or as a finger sandwich. The next day, after the social occasion has passed, friend and foe alike will consume whatever remains, if they know you have it in the refrigerator.

I have always heard it is a tricky recipe to make and even trickier to describe, as there is a fine line between just right and too runny. I find Benedictine easy to make but I have made a mess of it if I felt rushed. Just add the cucumber juice slowly and watch the consistency because you will want Benedictine creamy. If you feel the need to add some small amount of cucumber and onion pulp, then add it. I do not, but others do so, and if you do, add the cucumber and onion pulp very sparingly. There is no substitute for Philadelphia cream cheese.

INGREDIENTS
2 large cucumbers, peeled
1 medium white onion, peeled
2-8-oz. packages Philadelphia cream cheese
food coloring, green

DIRECTIONS

✔ In a blender separately grind the cucumber and the onion into pulp. Separately, place the pulp of each into a hand held fine mesh strainer. Gently press the pulp into small bowls until you have accumulated most of the juice. You now have a bowl of cucumber juice and a bowl of onion juice. I discard the pulp.
✔ Place the cream cheese into a mixer at slow speed.
✔ Gradually, add in juice from the cucumber. When you are satisfied the Benedictine is nice and creamy, add in about 1/2 of the juice from the onion.
✔ Then add 2 drops of green food coloring. If your eye says add more, then add 1 more. If your eye tells you to add 1 more after that, don't do it. The ideal color is peeled cucumber green
Serves 12-15 as an appetizer.

42. Pecan Chicken Salad

You will never make enough of this salad. I have served pecan chicken salad on toast as a sandwich, over lettuce and peeled tomatoes as a luncheon salad, in the summertime as the dinner entrée and as an appetizer with crackers.

I have watched polite company scooping it, bulk fashion onto their plate from the appetizer plate, leaving the crackers as refugees and eating it with a fork.

I have watched this same polite company making clandestine raids into the kitchen to find the bowl it was made in, attacking the pecan chicken salad with a spoon.

Similarly, I have watched this same polite company study the lay of the land, decide upon a point of interception and ambush the serving help attempting to cart the pecan chicken salad appetizer from kitchen to table.

Shameless behavior, I admit. However, it is not new to my generation; my mother and grandmother witnessed a similar reaction to pecan chicken salad.

Sweet pickle juice is used in the pecan chicken salad. It sounds bizarre but take it from me, it works. Mama Sudie and Sue Carol, always with an eye cast to making a great recipe better, introduced sweet pickle juice to me many years ago and I adopted it as my own.

There is no substitute for fresh boiled chicken breast.

INGREDIENTS

4 chicken breasts, boiled cooked, then skin, debone and cube
1 C Hellmann's mayonnaise
1/2 C pecans, chopped
1/2 C seedless white grapes, half cut
1/2 C celery, chopped
3 T sweet pickle juice
1 lemon, fresh squeezed
pepper, ground
salt

DIRECTIONS

✔ Place all ingredients in a bowl and mix with a wooden spoon. Add a touch more mayonnaise, if that is your preference. Grind pepper and salt to taste.

Serves 12-15, if an appetizer. Serves 6, if sandwiches. Serves 4, if a salad for luncheon or dinner.

43. Bourbon Cheese

Sunday afternoon in the cold of winter is a special time for our household. The evening comes early. The fireplaces are ablaze and glowing candles are on the table. Neighbors drop in and the drinking lamp is lit. A fine aged Kentucky bourbon whisky is poured and the bourbon cheese and crackers are placed on the end tables.

INGREDIENTS

8 oz. sharp cheddar cheese
8 oz. cream cheese
1/4 C fine aged Kentucky bourbon whisky
1/2 C pecans, chopped fine
1/4 C parsley, chopped
3 T onion, grated
1-t Worcestershire Sauce
1/4-t salt
1/4-t pepper, white
4 dashes Tabasco Sauce

DIRECTIONS

✔ Combine all ingredients in a mixer on slow speed. When the cheese appears to be thoroughly blended, form into a ball and place in a covered container. Refrigerate overnight.

44. Country Ham or Turkey Breast Biscuit

There are many ways to enjoy Country ham. The Kentucky way is to place two slices on a beaten biscuit, or an angel biscuit. We like the Country ham plain but we often place a bowl of Hellmann's mayonnaise or Durkee's dressing next to the Country ham for those requiring something extra.

Arranged on a platter, this is the quintessential pick up entrée and I do love it so. When securing a good Country ham is impossible, use slices of turkey breast. Not nearly as outstanding but good, and after all "one does what one can."

When I entertain a large group, I almost always serve a platter both of Country ham and turkey breast on beaten biscuit or angel biscuits.

45. Bourbon Balls

The bourbon ball is a piece of the fabric that forms the Kentucky hospitality tapestry. Bourbon balls are presented at times as an appetizer, occasionally as a dessert and often on coffee tables when the drinks are being poured.

When I am sipping fine aged Kentucky bourbon whisky and our company is graced by the presence of a number of women on a warm, breezy day, I try to make the passing of bourbon balls a studied ritual. Women seem to adore bourbon balls and after all is said I do seem to spend much of my life striving to make the women happy.

Your guests will go crazy when they taste bourbon balls. Keep the recipe handy; they will ask you for it.

INGREDIENTS

1 C pecans, chopped
1/2 C fine aged Kentucky bourbon whisky
1/2 C butter
2 # white powdered sugar
4 oz. semi sweet chocolate, bits
1 square bar paraffin

DIRECTIONS

✔ Soak the pecans in a fine-aged Kentucky bourbon whisky for 1 hour.

✔ In a bowl, combine the butter, sugar, and pecans; knead by hand until blended. Add in any of the remaining bourbon. Make into 1-inch balls.

✔ In a double boiler, simmering hot, not boiling, mix the chocolate bits and the paraffin. Stir the chocolate bits and the paraffin with a wooden spoon until melted together.

✔ Then dip each bourbon ball in the chocolate and paraffin mixture with a wooden spoon and thoroughly coat.

✔ Place on wax paper until cool, then refrigerate in a covered container.

46. Stuffed Mushrooms

Stuffed mushrooms are a standard on the serving tables of Kentucky homes. I have served them most often in the summer for large gatherings on the lawn. However, I have seen stuffed mushrooms on the sideboards of many homes in all seasons.

INGREDIENTS

12 oz. hot breakfast sausage
1 C sharp cheddar cheese, shredded
1/2 C bread crumbs, finely rolled
2 T parsley, chopped fine
1/4-t pepper, red flakes
24-30 medium to large mushrooms, stems removed, forming a bowl

DIRECTIONS

✔ Blend all of the ingredients by hand. When completely blended stuff each mushroom with a heaping amount of stuffing and place them on a well oiled baking sheet in such a way that they do not "lopsize."

✔ Bake at 375 degrees for 45 minutes and serve immediately.

Serves 8-10.

47. Salted Walnuts

I enjoy salted peanuts as much as the next man, dry roasted and red skins are my favorite. If, however, you will make a decision to do your own, salted walnuts are a fine choice.

INGREDIENTS

4 C walnuts, shelled and left whole
1 T butter
1 T salt

DIRECTIONS

✔ Place walnuts in a bowl. Drizzle the butter over the walnuts and swoosh around until completely covered. Mix in the salt making certain all of the walnuts, have equal coverage. Arrange walnuts on a dry baking sheet so that there is no overlapping.

✔ Bake at 275 degrees for 30 minutes.

48. Sausage Balls

I have never seen a sausage ball outside of Kentucky, which probably means I do not get away from the house as much as I should. They are simple and delicious. Be patient and persistently work the mixture. Mixing the ingredients together always takes longer than I think it should.

INGREDIENTS

1 # hot breakfast sausage
1/2 # mild breakfast sausage
1 C sharp cheddar cheese, shredded
6 C Bisquick

DIRECTIONS

✔ Mix the cheese and the sausage by hand. Add the flour a cup at a time, again working the mixture by hand. Form into balls about the size of large marbles. After forming into balls, the sausage balls may be frozen for later use.

✔ Bake at 350 degrees until golden brown, about 45 minutes, watching that they do not get over cooked, as they will get hard. If previously frozen, add about 10 minutes to the cooking time. Yields 75 sausage balls.

49. Cheese Straws

INGREDIENTS

2 C sharp cheddar cheese
6 T butter, melted
1 C flour, sifted
2-t baking powder
1-t pepper cayenne

DIRECTIONS

✔ Cream the cheese and butter in a mixer at slow speed. Mix in the remaining ingredients. Place on a cutting board, pat down more or less flat and cut into 4-inch long straws.

✔ Place on a well oiled baking sheet, spaced so as not touching. Bake at 325 degrees for about 25 minutes or until they are crisp and dry.

Again, your guests will eat as many as you bake.

Breads

I have spent a lifetime making friends with the baking arts. Just as I think I have learned something, it disappears on my next attempt. Maybe it is my heavy hand or a lack of sensitivity or the planets are aligned against me.

I decided many years ago to bake four great breads: breakfast biscuits, yeast rolls, angel biscuits and beaten biscuit. When people light at McManus House they will be served one of these breads; if they stay the weekend they will probably sample all four.

Yeast rolls are my favorite bread to bake. They are easy to prepare, once you have an experience with them. I often make the dough the night before their use and place the dough in the refrigerator. The trick is to learn what I mean by bubbly yeast.

When you prepare yeast rolls, you will lose your last days of peace upon this earth. You will be expected to bake these yeast rolls when company travels to your house. That same company will invite you to their home, and when you ask, "What can I bring?" they will tell you yeast rolls.

Yeast rolls are a Kentucky thing. I find them on good Kentucky tables but rarely outside of Kentucky. I have surmised that our distilling industry, practiced by many in the backshed, afforded us a continuous supply of yeast and an active interest in the fine bread it produced. The cook who can master these rolls can build a career on the applause. I have neighbors who would fall out with me if I made yeast rolls without sending some over.

I am telling you straight, if you would allow it, folk high and low will make a meal out of yeast rolls. They are that good.

Baking times will vary according to the size of the roll you are baking and the accuracy of the oven. When Margaret Sue and I purchased a new oven, my old times needed adjustment. Just attend to the rolls. Golden brown is the color my eye is seeking.

50. Breakfast Biscuit

This recipe is an excellent baking powder biscuit. The recipe calls for cream of tartar, a very old method used to enhance the rise. Be gentle with these biscuits. My family laughed at my first attempts many years ago, attributing my lackluster results to my heavy hand, which is the size of a bear paw. A grandmotherly friend told me to handle the dough as if holding a baby's hand. Since having that as a mental image I have been successful with the breakfast biscuit.

This piece of advice is experience, not science—cut the biscuit straight down and do not twist the biscuit cutter, otherwise the biscuit will tend to lopsize. These biscuits are very easy to make but be kind to yourself, make them in private the first time out, so you can get the feel of them.

If some are left over, cover them with tin foil the next morning, halve them, put a small pat of butter on each half and broil. Heaven.

INGREDIENTS
3 C flour
3/4-t salt
3/4-t cream of tartar
1 T plus 1-1/2-t baking powder
2-t sugar
3/4 C shortening
3/4 C milk
1 egg, beaten

DIRECTIONS

✔ In a large bowl, gently, stir in the dry ingredients of flour, salt, tartar, baking powder and sugar with a wooden spoon.
Add the shortening, cutting it in with a pastry knife until the texture is pebbly and coarse.

✔ Mix the milk and egg together with a whisk. Pour onto the flour and quickly but gently stir into the dough with the wooden spoon.

✔ The dough is ready when it follows the spoon around the bowl.

✔ Turn out the dough onto a lightly, and I do mean lightly, floured table. Knead 6-8 times, lightly and gently, folding the dough over itself. Roll to 1-inch thickness, cut into 2-inch biscuits. Place on a dry baking sheet.

✔ Bake at 450 degrees for 15 minutes or until tops are browned.

51. Yeast Rolls

INGREDIENTS
2 C flour, sifted,
1/2 C flour, sifted at the ready for dusting
1/2 C milk or sour cream
1/4 C water (lukewarm, 110 degrees)
2 T sugar
1/2 t salt
2 T butter
1 egg, beaten
1 package dry yeast
Yield 10-12 rolls

52. Yeast Rolls

INGREDIENTS
5-1/2 C flour, sifted,
1/2 C flour, sifted at the ready for dusting
2 C milk or sour cream
1/4 C water (lukewarm, 110 degrees)
2 T sugar
2-t salt
2 T butter
1 egg, beaten
1 package dry yeast
Yield 25-30 rolls

DIRECTIONS

✔ Heat the milk in a pan until it almost comes to a boil, then cut off the heat.

✔ Add the sugar, salt and butter and let the mixture cool until lukewarm. This will take about 10 minutes. When lukewarm add in the egg. Set aside.

✔ Warm a mixing bowl by running warm water over the inside and outside, then dry with a cloth. Place the yeast into the bowl and add the water and stir until you are convinced the yeast is dissolved. Let stand until it is bubbly, about 20 minutes.

✔ Pour the milk or sour cream, sugar, salt, butter and egg into the mixing bowl and combine with the yeast.

✔ Add 1/2 C of flour in the mixing bowl and beat the dough for 3-4 minutes with a wooden spoon, making certain you include the sides and bottom of the bowl. Add the remaining flour and beat for 3-4 minutes.

✔ Cover the bowl with a damp cloth and allow dough to rise in a warm place, about 80-85 degrees, until doubled in bulk, which will take about an hour and a half.

✔ When the dough has doubled, if the dough is to be used the following day, cover the bowl and place in the refrigerator. If using the dough the same day, release the dough upon a table, which has been dusted lightly.

✔ Knead the dough with flour-dusted hands by bringing the far edge of the dough toward the center and pressing in the center of the dough gently with the heel of your hand. The idea is to knead the dough without pressing out the gases generated by the active yeast. Turn the dough and repeat the kneading procedure. If you need to dust the table again to prevent sticking, then do so. Knead the dough until the underside is smooth and silky.

✔ Then place the dough on a lightly-dusted table. Press the dough from the center with your hands in all four directions, then using a lightly dusted rolling pin, gently but quickly roll out the dough from the center in all directions. Be careful never to roll past the edge of the dough. Lightly dust the top and the bottom of the dough as needed to prevent sticking.

"Kentucky"

In the heart of old Kentucky,
Where the grass is always green,
Where the bees are ever working,
Making honey for their queen,
There the sheep and lowing cattle
Gladly graze in pastures wide
To say, "I'm from that good old State,"
Sure fills me up with pride.

For pretty women, loyal hearts,
And horses fleet of foot,
Kentucky produces more of these
Than all States to boot.
For hospitality reigns supreme,
Her people's hearts are wide.
To say, "I'm from that good old State,"
Sure fills me up with pride.

– **H. E. Folsom**, *in*
The Louisville Evening Post

53. Dinner Rolls

DIRECTIONS

✔ Roll the yeast dough 1/2-inch thick. Cut with a 2-inch biscuit cutter or a tumbler. Crease the dough across the middle and fold over for effect. Brush the top of the rolls with butter. Place the rolls in an oiled baking pan.

✔ Cover the pan with a damp cloth and allow the rolls to rise in a warm place until doubled in bulk, about 30 minutes.

✔ Bake at 400 degrees for 12-20 minutes, or until golden brown.

54. Clover Leaf Rolls

DIRECTIONS

✔ Roll the yeast dough to 1/2-inch thick. Pinch off a piece and roll it into a marble size ball. Dip each ball in melted butter and place three in an oiled muffin pan.

✔ Cover the pan with a damp cloth and allow the rolls to rise in a warm place until doubled in bulk, about 30 minutes.

✔ Bake at 400 degrees for 12-20 minutes or until golden brown.

55. Butterscotch Breakfast Sweet Rolls

DIRECTIONS

✔ Roll the yeast dough 1/4-inch thick, brush the dough with softened butter and sprinkle 1/2 C brown sugar on the buttered dough. Roll the dough up from the long side. Brush the top and the sides of the rolled up dough with butter. Cut into 3/4-inch pieces.

✔ Melt 4 T of butter in oiled baking pan and cover the butter with 3/4 C brown sugar. Sprinkle mixture with chopped pecans. Place rolls close together, face down in the butter.

✔ Cover the pan with a damp cloth and allow the rolls to rise in a warm place until doubled in bulk, about 30 minutes.

✔ Bake at 400 degrees for 12-20 minutes or until golden brown.

✔ After baking, upend the pan onto a plate and allow the butter-brown sugar-pecan mixture to seep down into the roll for a minute and liberate rolls.

56. Cinnamon Rolls

I have attended many a feeding frenzy when cinnamon rolls are on the breakfast table. Young people seem to like these rolls with more sugar than I have offered in this recipe. When more sugar seems to be good politics dissolve 1/2 C of brown sugar to 1/2 stick butter and spread upon the rolled out dough.

DIRECTIONS

✔ Roll dough to 1/4-inch thick, and brush the top of the dough with softened butter.

✔ Prepare a mixture of 1/4 C sugar and 2-t cinnamon and sprinkle it evenly across the top of the dough.

✔ Roll up the dough from the long side and pinch the edge so as to seal in the cinnamon and sugar.

✔ Cut the roll into 3/4-inch pieces.

✔ Place the rolls into an oiled baking pan with the sides lightly touching.

✔ Cover the pan with a damp cloth and allow the rolls to rise in a warm place until doubled in bulk, about 30 minutes.

✔ Bake at 400 degrees for 12-20 minutes, or until golden brown.

57. Cinnamon Rolls Icing

DIRECTIONS

✔ Bring 4 T Half and Half or milk almost to a boil, add in enough powdered sugar to make a good spreading consistency.

✔ Stir with a wooden spoon until the sugar is dissolved.

✔ Flavor with 1/2-t vanilla.

✔ Spread the icing over the tops of the cinnamon rolls as they come out of the oven.

58. Angel Biscuits

When the prospect of making beaten biscuit leaves you cold and the baker never seems to have a truly great small roll for the sliced ham and turkey, angel biscuits are the answer. They are easy to make and wonderful.

The rolls can be made a day ahead of time, if you will place them in the refrigerator, covered with a cloth. When you are ready to use them, remove from the refrigerator and let stand for 10 minutes. Keep an eye on them; you do not want them to rise.

INGREDIENTS
5 C flour
2 C buttermilk
3/4 C vegetable shortening
1/2 C water (lukewarm, 110 degrees)
3 T sugar
1 T baking powder
1-t salt
1-t baking soda
1 pkg. yeast

DIRECTIONS

✔ Dissolve yeast in the water with 1 T of the sugar and set to the side.

✔ In a large bowl, combine flour, sugar, salt, baking powder, baking soda and stir gently with a wooden spoon. Cut in shortening with a pastry knife until dough is coarse and pebbly. Add yeast and buttermilk and stir gently with the wooden spoon.

✔ Take a second large bowl and coat the inside of the bowl with shortening. Transfer the dough to this second bowl and turn the dough around the inside of the bowl until the outside of the dough is lightly coated. This will keep a crust from forming.

✔ Roll the dough to 1/2-inch and cut with a small diameter biscuit cutter, in the absence of small diameter biscuit cutter, a whiskey jigger will suffice.

✔ Bake at 400 degrees for 12 minutes.

59. Beaten Biscuit

I have fond memories of my grandparents and my father and mother making these biscuits in very large quantities for an upcoming party. The beaten biscuit is a roll that brings out the best flavor of ham and turkey. I usually make the beaten biscuit on the Thursday night prior to a Saturday party. Make plenty; if you have some left over they make delicious buttered toast for Sunday breakfast. The old way is to use lard for the shortening; I use vegetable shortening for reasons that are obvious to me.

The making of beaten biscuit calls for it to be rolled through a biscuit brake. If you know the biscuit brake and would like to obtain one, write to me. I will see if I can find one or give you the name of a company that can make one for you.

Alternately, you can make beaten biscuit by rolling the dough out with a rolling pin. The dough should be rolled out to 1 inch then folded north to south, rolled again to 1 inch thick and then repeated continuously until the dough pops.

Regardless of the method utilized for rolling out the beaten biscuit dough, the idea is to make the dough blister and pop, a sign that the dough has trapped the air.

The old way—when without a biscuit break—was to beat the dough with a rolling pin hundreds of times for your family and hundreds more for company. Sounds charming, but I am not inclined to that work. I have experimented with rolling the dough with success in my effort to imitate the biscuit break.

I realize that only the most flinty-eyed cook will go to the trouble of rolling dough until it blisters, but it is worth it and to my mind, very satisfying. Hopefully, you will discover the charm and grace in making a biscuit that has been enjoyed in Kentucky for hundreds of years. Pour a fine aged Kentucky bourbon whisky about half way through the dough rolling enterprise. If your courage fails, you can always bake angel biscuits to put up with your ham and turkey. But as for beaten biscuit here you have it.

INGREDIENTS

3 C flour, sifted twice with the baking powder and salt
1-t salt
1-t baking powder
1/4 C vegetable shortening
1/2 C whole milk

DIRECTIONS

✔ Place the flour in a large bowl and cut in the shortening with a pastry knife until coarse and pebbly.
✔ Combine the milk, salt and baking powder.
✔ Add the milk to the flour and shortening and stir with a wooden spoon, add more milk if you must but add it by the teaspoon until the dough makes a good firm ball. Turn the dough onto a lightly floured table and knead until dough is firm, dry and elastic.

✔ Now the fun begins. This next step is a procedure requiring a partner. Run the dough through the biscuit brake, folding the dough over itself after each pass through the rollers until it pops and is silky smooth.
✔ Alternately use the rolling pin.
✔ Roll dough out to a 1-inch thickness; cut dough with a small biscuit cutter. Arrange biscuits on a dry baking pan, sides touching and prick each biscuit with a fork 4 times, the fork being allowed to touch the pan as it goes through.
✔ Bake at 350 degrees for 30-35 minutes or until lightly browned on top.

Place on counter until cooled. Place the biscuits, after they have cooled in a tight container and they will keep perfectly for several days. Plan on 2-3 biscuits for each guest.

Meat/Vegetable Sauces and Salad Dressings

I have a dozen good meat/vegetable sauces and salad dressings that dominate my cooking. I use them frequently and often. My wife, Margaret Sue, and I have a feud that started with our marriage and has lasted to this day over sauces. Margaret Sue feels I should increase the range and scope of my sauces and dressings. I defer to her judgment in most matters relating to style but fight her fearlessly on sauces and dressings. I find pleasure in preparing certain sauces and dressings and therefore, stand my turf.

It is a cooking imperative that you taste any sauce or dressing that you prepare. When you have completed your sauce or dressing, by all means, taste it. This is an area in cooking where your opinion really matters. The addition of some salt or pepper or a little more thickening can make a world of difference to the final outcome.

I have a decided preference for using sauces and dressings lightly. When you purchase the best quality meats and produce, you have the essential ingredients for an outstanding dining experience. The sauces and dressings are presented to enhance the great tastes of those foods. Therefore, I tend to place the amount I think is correct upon the food and leave a bowl on the side for those that prefer more.

60. Masters Steak Sauce

If you do not have a steak sauce that you can claim, use this sauce. I have been making up sauce recipes for years and I love this one. What is the secret ingredient? Somebody, somewhere, told me to try ginger in my sauce. I did and the rest is history. Masters Steak Sauce will keep indefinitely when refrigerated, although at my gatherings it is inhaled, the bowl scraped clean.

Masters Steak Sauce is used on all premium steak cuts but reaches majesty on rare beef: prime rib and tenderloin. It is the reason we cook baby back ribs. As a dressing for grilled or broiled ground meats, it is divine. We have also drizzled it on Bibb lettuce salads, and used it to flavor green beans with great success. That tells me folks will take Masters Steak Sauce anyway they can get it.

Many a time I have been standing at the grill at McManus House with a gallery of folk around me when the question comes, "May I taste your sauce?" Long ago I learned to place Benedictine, pimento cheese and crackers in close proximity to the grill. That way a fellow can dip a cracker and I do not have to suffer a finger dragged around the bowl wherein dwells my Masters Steak Sauce.

I have seen many a man taste Masters Steak Sauce on a cracker. His next foray into the sauce is with a cracker loaded down with Benedictine and pimento cheese. Makes sense to me. Done it myself.

I almost always double the recipe for Masters Steak Sauce. This sauce disappears quickly at McManus House.

INGREDIENTS

1-1/4 C tomato sauce
3/4 C red wine vinegar
1/2 C brown sugar
2 T dry mustard
1 T powdered or grated ginger
2-t pepper
2-t salt
1-t garlic powder
3 T olive oil
1 lemon, whole, fresh squeezed
1 T fine aged Kentucky bourbon whisky

DIRECTIONS

✔ Combine all ingredients except the olive oil, lemon and bourbon. Simmer for 20 minutes, stirring with whisk.

✔ Turn off the heat and stir in the olive oil, lemon and bourbon. Let Masters Steak Sauce cool in the pan for about 30 minutes. This will allow the vinegar and bourbon to settle down. Cover and refrigerate overnight to blend the flavors. I find the sauce especially good on the third day.

61. Bourbon Cheese Sauce

We have served our bourbon cheese sauce over asparagus, broccoli and cauliflower for many years. I often steer around Hollandaise sauce, mainly because I find this too delicate for entertaining a large group when I am doing the cooking, drinking a fine-aged Kentucky bourbon whisky, enjoying my friends and not having a precise dinner schedule.

INGREDIENTS

1 C sharp cheddar cheese, grated
1/2 C Half and Half
1/4 C butter
2-t fresh lemon juice
parsley, chopped
4 dashes fine aged Kentucky bourbon whisky
pepper, ground

DIRECTIONS

✔ Place the cheese in a pan. Add the Half and Half and the butter. Stir the sauce on a low heat with a whisk until it is creamy.

✔ Add the lemon juice, parsley and bourbon whisky. Grind pepper onto the sauce.

62. Hollandaise Sauce

INGREDIENTS

1/2 C butter
2 egg yolk, beaten
1 T lemon juice, fresh
1/4 C water, in the lower pan
1/4-t salt
pepper, ground

DIRECTIONS

✔ Using a double boiler, bring water in lower pan to a simmer.

✔ In upper pan, melt one half of the butter, add the egg, and the lemon juice. Stir constantly with a whisk. When sauce begins to thicken, add the remaining butter. As this thickens, add the boiling water. When the mixture is thickened once again, season with the salt and pepper.

✔ If the sauce separates add boiling water, drop by drop, stirring with the whisk.

"Back Home"

Will I meet you at the banquet board,
When those who are so lucky
Will greet old friends and meet new friends,
And talk about Kentucky?
Of coarse I will, for to each heart,
No matter where we roam,
Among this crowd, hand clasped in hand,
We feel once more "Back Home."

No other State so clannish as
this dear one of ours,
With its bluegrass and fine horses,
and its women sweet as flowers;
And when we get together and
Kentucky whisky flows,
There is a kindred spirit
On other State e'er knows.

Written for the Kentucky Colonels Club,
Dallas, Texas,
October, 1915

63. Lobster Sauce

Add to Hollandaise 1/2 C finely chopped lobster. It is a wonderful sauce on broccoli, cauliflower and asparagus. We love to serve it on premier cuts of filet of fish such as swordfish or salmon.

64. Horseradish Sauce

Add to Hollandaise 4 T grated horseradish and 2 T heavy cream to the sauce as it is removed from the heat. Stir briskly with the whisk until the sauce has stiffened. A real good complement to buttered lamb chops and rare filet of beef.

65. Béarnaise Sauce

Add to Hollandaise 1-t each of fine chopped parsley and tarragon. It is a classic with rare beef. We like it best on strip steak that has been grilled with the upper side heavily coated with coarse black pepper.

66. Chives Sauce

Add to Hollandaise chives or finely chopped spring onion (bulb and upper leaves). Pour over new potatoes.

67. Sour Cream Dressing

The sour cream dressing is a favorite of Margaret Sue's and this is a recipe she favors. I have always found that egg based sauces tax my patience. Margaret Sue prepares sour cream dressing for asparagus and when she does I am her most enthusiastic supporter. Like Hollandaise sauce, it is a trick to make it in quantities required for a large group and, therefore, lends the making of it to a dinner of two or three couples, making sour cream sauce a product of Margaret Sue's domain.

INGREDIENTS

2 egg yolk, beaten
1 C sour cream
1 T lemon juice
1-t salt
1/4-t dry mustard
1/4-t sugar
Tabasco Sauce to taste

DIRECTIONS

✔ In a mixing bowl and using a whisk, blend the egg yolks and the sour cream.

✔ Add the remaining ingredients and stir them into the mixture.

✔ Using a double boiler on a simmering boil, heat the sauce very gently, stirring continuously with the whisk. The dressing will curdle if it gets too much heat.

68. Basic Cream Sauce

If there is a sauce that can be used a hundred different ways, it would have to be cream sauce. There are chefs around the world that spend a lifetime perfecting their cream sauces. I advocate the learning of the basic cream sauce and in this sauce is the foundation for dozens of interesting flavors. Let your imagination lead you to a couple of cream sauces you enjoy and by all means, name one after yourself.

The basic cream sauce is a wedding of butter, cream and flour. Remembering that milk products deteriorate under heat, be kind to the sauce and just simmer it.

The basic cream sauce is: 1 C Half and Half, 3 T butter, 3 T flour, 1/4-t salt and ground pepper.

DIRECTIONS

✔ Place the Half and Half in a pan, add the butter and stir with a whisk under a low heat. Stir in the flour. When you are satisfied that the cream sauce is well blended, if thickening is deemed desirable, add a small amount of cornstarch dissolved in a small amount of warm water, gradually. Stir the cream sauce with a whisk under a low simmering heat until it is of a consistency you require. Add the salt and ground pepper.

I enjoy the taste and visual appeal of herbs, especially on sauces. I often sprinkle parsley and basil on top of the sauce and do not hesitate to use chives and spring onion.

Be creative. Your guests will love it.

There is a simple elegance that I admire inherent in the basic cream sauce. I use this sauce on fowl of any kind, filet of fish and numerous pasta and vegetable dishes. As it might suit your purpose, flavor the sauce with fresh lemon, lime or paprika. Tabasco Sauce finds a place on occasion.

Prepare lima beans, boiled or baked onions, green peas, zucchini squash or cauliflower. Pour basic cream sauce over your vegetable of choice and toss gently. Serve immediately.

69. Mushroom Sauce

Add sautéed mushrooms to the basic cream sauce for use on filet of beef or chicken breast.

70. Almond Sauce

Sauté slivered almonds and add to the basic cream sauce to complement fish and fowl.

71. Egg Sauce

Add a lightly beaten egg yolk to the basic cream sauce, stir in with a whisk over a low heat. Serve over broccoli and cauliflower. Sprinkle the top with paprika.

72. Cheese Sauce

Add grated mild cheddar cheese to the basic cream sauce and add fresh lemon or lime juice, if you like. The combination is good on all manner of steamed vegetables.

We like this sauce on open-faced club sandwiches. To toast, add a thick, peeled tomato slice, lettuce, four strips of cooked bacon, and give the sandwich a good covering of cheese sauce. Pour on Masters Steak Sauce for a powerfully great Sunday breakfast treat.

73. Clam Sauce

Add clam liquor to the basic cream sauce to create a wonderful sauce over pasta noodles or filet of fish. Add anchovy paste for accent. If you enjoy clams and, if or when, they are cooked, mince them and stir them into the sauce.

74. Shrimp Sauce

Add a good quantity of cooked and cleaned whole shrimp to the basic cream sauce. Pour the sauce over egg noodles. Sprinkle poppy seed and grind black pepper over the sauce.

75. Scallop Sauce

Steam scallops and place into a serving bowl. Squeeze half a lemon over the scallops. Pour the basic cream sauce over the scallops. Pour the sauce over egg noodles. Sprinkle the sauce liberally with fresh chopped parsley and spring onion. Grind black pepper onto the sauce.

76. Brown Mushroom Sauce

I use the brown mushroom sauce for buttered lamb chops and roasts of beef.

INGREDIENTS
basic cream sauce
butter
mushrooms, sliced thin
red wine or sherry
1 T onion, finely chopped
drippings or beef bouillon

DIRECTIONS

✔ Prepare the basic cream sauce and set aside.

✔ In a pan sauté thinly sliced mushrooms in butter and a small amount of red wine or sherry until the mushrooms are tender.

✔ In another pan, sauté butter and a tablespoon of finely chopped onion over a medium high heat until the butter and the onion are of a good brown color.

✔ Use some of the drippings from a prepared red meat or use a dissolved beef bouillon cube and add to the cream mixture. Stir in with a whisk.

✔ Add the mushrooms and the onion and allow the brown mushroom sauce to slowly simmer, all the while stirring with the whisk.

77. Vinaigrette

Simple to make, you will use this basic dressing for lettuce based salads and cold marinated asparagus. We include crumbled blue cheese, feta, and other dry cheeses when it suits our fancy, making the vinaigrette a good foundation salad and vegetable dressing.

Sliced cucumbers, tomatoes and red onion, marinated for an hour in vinaigrette, is terrific. We love this salad in the heat of summer. It can be made in large quantity for a barbecue or picnic.

I often find myself amazed that vinaigrette is such a fine marinade for meats and over the years have made multiple and various uses of it.

INGREDIENTS

2-1/2 T lemon juice, fresh squeezed
2 cloves garlic, minced
1 C olive oil
1-1/2 T white vinegar
2-t salt
1-t pepper, ground

DIRECTIONS

✔ Place the squeezed lemon juice in a bowl; scrape the lemon pulp into the bowl. Add the garlic. Let stand for about an hour.
✔ Pour the mixture through a hand held fine mesh strainer into a mixing bowl.
✔ Then, using a whisk, mix in the olive oil, vinegar, salt and ground pepper. Cover and refrigerate until ready to serve.

78. French Dressing

We use French dressing on Bibb lettuce and spinach salads. We also enjoy it on grapefruit and orange slices. Refrigerate overnight to blend the flavors. Some like to retain a portion of the onion, I do not.

INGREDIENTS
1/2 C olive oil
1/2 orange, juiced
1/2 lemon, juiced
1 T parsley, finely chopped
1 T onion, finely chopped
1-t Worcestershire Sauce
1-t onion salt
1/4-t mustard powder
1/4-t paprika

DIRECTIONS

✔ Combine all of the ingredients and mix well with a whisk.

✔Cover and refrigerate one day to blend the flavors. Pour the dressing through a hand held fine mesh strainer into a bowl to capture the onion, which you will discard.

79. Thousand Island Dressing

INGREDIENTS
1 C Hellmann's mayonnaise
1/4 C chili sauce
2 hard boiled eggs, chopped fine
2 T spring onion, chopped fine
2 T green pepper, chopped fine
2 T Half and Half
1-t Worcestershire Sauce

DIRECTIONS

✔ Blend the mayonnaise and the chili sauce with a whisk.

✔ Then one at a time, stir in the eggs, onion, green pepper.

✔ Add the Half and Half and the Worcestershire Sauce and stir for several minutes with the whisk.

✔ Refrigerate and serve chilled.

Salads

Every meal, in my opinion, benefits from a salad. I like to serve mixtures of fruits at any meal in a big bowl or on a bed of Bibb lettuce or spinach leaves. I combine Bibb lettuce and spinach with fruit for luncheon and dinner.

Several slices of pineapple cut fresh with a dab of smearcase is elegant. Melons and fresh blueberries are wonderful. Strawberries and blackberries are an early summer treat. The trick is to use fresh fruit and avoid the syrupy mess canned fruit is immersed in. My one exception is mandarin oranges; I buy them in the can.

One of the more irritating vexations in life, as far as I am concerned, is a warm salad, intentional or otherwise. I like chilled salads. I have not tasted a warm salad that ever appealed to me. To the extent that I can, I make my salads ahead of time so they may cool in the refrigerator. I even go so far as to place my lettuce in a colander, setting the colander in a bowl and layering ice cubes across the top to achieve maximum chilling effect. I withhold the dressing until time to serve.

80. Mixed Green Salad

The mixed green salad used in our entertaining is a meal unto itself. I serve it in all seasons, but find it especially attractive as an early Sunday dinner.

When we are entertaining people we know from central Kentucky we use a cheese made by the cloistered friars of Gethsemane Abbey that they call Trappist Cheese and we affectionately call Monk's Cheese. The cheese is absolutely strong as to taste and absolutely pungent and sour in aroma. Those of us who have grown up around the Gethsemane Abbey, just south of Bardstown, have an appreciation for their cheeses and bourbon-soaked fruitcakes. The bourbon-soaked fruitcakes have found a loyal clientele and is a product that is exported all over the world as the best of its kind. Monk's Cheese, however, I fear, is an acquired affinity and therefore I offer feta cheese as an acceptable substitution.

Margaret Sue likes tarragon as an additional spice, I like basil and chives. McManus House is an American household and we tend to accommodate both of our preferences and use all three, thereby circumventing a challenge. The herb garden, grown outside the back door, is kept well clipped by our usage of it.

Use 8 ounces of beef tenderloin or two chicken breasts. Sauté one or the other in butter until the beef tenderloin is medium rare or the chicken breast is cooked throughout. Slice the beef or the chicken on the diagonal, thin, keeping the pieces as long as you can.

INGREDIENTS
5 C mixed young lettuce
5 eggs, hard boiled
1 C red onion, diced
6 oz. feta cheese
2 tomatoes, peeled and quartered
tarragon
basil
chives
pepper, ground
vinaigrette dressing
8 ounces beef tenderloin or two chicken breast fillets

DIRECTIONS

✔ **Combine the lettuce and the hard boiled eggs and divide the lettuce among four dinner plates.**

✔ **Sprinkle the lettuce on each plate with the red onion and the feta cheese.**

✔ **Garnish the sides of each plate with the quartered tomatoes.**

✔ **Season with tarragon, basil, chives and pepper to taste.**

✔ **Place 3-4 beef tenderloin or chicken breast strips on top of the salad.**

✔ **Pour the vinaigrette dressing over the salad.**

"Our Own Kentucky Girl"

Other girls may have their graces,
Charms, attractions and all that;
Some may shine in silks and laces,
Or the latest Paris hat;
But the one who queens all others,
Makes them all their banners furl –
You'll all agree my brothers –
Is our own Kentucky girl.

She's as fair as springtime morning,
She's as joyous as a lark;
She can conquer without warning,
When she deigns to hit the mark
In the field of high endeavor,
Or the placing of a curl –
Ah, she's "chic" and sweet and clever,
Is our own Kentucky girl.

She can ride and swim and tango,
Play bridge, whist or shoot, or walk;
Make preserves of peach and mango,
Charm all hearers with her talk;
Has a heart that thinks no evil,
Is herself like choicest pearl –
Confound mankind or the devil,
Can our own Kentucky girl.

She can comfort sad and weary,
Give surcease to any pain;
She's as sunshine to the dreary,
Brighter than chateau in Spain;
All things else that life might proffer
Rolled in one, I'd promptly hurl
To oblivion, should you offer
Them for our Kentucky girl.

– Alan Pegram Gilmour

81. McManus House Salad

There are times when only the most delicious salad I know of will suffice. McManus House salad is a salad I enjoy grazing upon. I am always regretful to find my bowl empty. This salad is strictly hammers back and ready.

The McManus House salad works well with a light entrée such as buttered lamb chops or a small cut of filet of beef. It can be made in good quantity for a seated dinner or luncheon of eight guests.

INGREDIENTS
2 C chicken breast, diced
2 head Bibb lettuce
1 head iceberg lettuce
1 stalk of romaine lettuce, inner leaves
1 C Thousand Island dressing
3/4 C blue cheese, crumbled
2 T white wine vinegar
tarragon
parsley
basil
ground black pepper
16 bacon slices, cooked

DIRECTIONS
✔ Shred the lettuce into bite-size pieces. Mix all of the ingredients together.
✔ Season with the tarragon, parsley, basil and ground pepper.
✔ Place the McManus House salad into eight bowls.
✔ Place two strips of shredded bacon on the top of each salad.

82. Red Potato Salad

INGREDIENTS
12 red potatoes, boiled
2 C sour cream
1 bunch green onion, onion bulb and green leaves, chopped
1 C celery, diced
1 T seasoning salt
2-t pepper

DIRECTIONS
✔ Allow the potatoes to cool and when cool quarter them.
✔ Coat the potatoes with the sour cream, tossing gently.
✔ Distribute the spring onion, celery, seasoning salt and pepper throughout the bowl and again, toss gently.
✔ Refrigerate the red potato salad overnight to blend flavors.

83. Spinach Salad

INGREDIENTS
8-oz. spinach leaves
1 medium red onion, sliced thin
8 bacon strips, cooked crisply and chopped fine
1 can mandarin oranges, drained
4 medium size mushrooms, fresh and sliced thin
1/4 C almonds, slivered
pepper, ground
French dressing

DIRECTIONS
✔ De-vein spinach leaves, wash in several cold waters, drain and dry thoroughly. Shred the spinach into reasonable pieces.
✔ In a mixing bowl combine all of the ingredients with the spinach leaves. Cover and refrigerate until time to serve.
✔ When ready for the table, mix in French dressing and toss until spinach leaves are moist. Grind pepper onto salad. This salad performs best when the dressing is used lightly.

84. Bibb Lettuce Salad

INGREDIENTS
3 heads of Bibb lettuce
1 grapefruit, peeled, sections removed
1 can mandarin oranges, drained
1 bunch spring onion, chopped up to the green leaves
French dressing
pepper, ground

DIRECTIONS

✔ **Place 6-8 Bibb lettuce leaves on each dinner plate or individual salad plate.**

✔ **Arrange grapefruit and mandarin oranges on top lettuce.**

✔ **Sprinkle on the spring onion.**

✔ **Pour on the French dressing, sparingly. Grind pepper onto salad.**

85. Smearcase

I have never seen smearcase outside of the Bluegrass region of Kentucky. It is a very elegant tomato topping. A bed of Bibb lettuce with thick sliced peeled tomatoes and smearcase is a great salad.

INGREDIENTS
1 qt. cottage cheese, large curd
1/4 C Hellmann's mayonnaise
2-bunches spring onions, bulb only, diced
ground pepper

DIRECTIONS

✔ **Combine the cottage cheese and the mayonnaise in a mixing bowl and blend at a slow speed. You will need to turn off the mixer several times and use a wooden spoon to bring the cottage cheese to the top.**

✔ **When blended, add the spring onion.**

✔ **Cover and refrigerate for eight hours.**

✔ **When ready to serve, grind black pepper across the top of the smearcase.**

86. Apple Salad

We often use fruit in our salads as a counterpoint to the meat we serve. I have always favored an inclination toward lemon and the natural sweet taste of fruit. Apple salad is another fine example of this tendency. Apple salad is used as a summer salad but we also like to place a nice spoonful next to roasted pork tenderloin and any of the wild birds we harvest in the fall and winter such as dove, duck and goose.

INGREDIENTS

6 Granny Smith apples, cut in slices and then cut in half
4 bananas, sliced medium thin
1 C dried cranberries
1 C walnuts, chopped coarse
1/2 C Hellmann's mayonnaise
1 lemon, fresh squeezed
pepper, ground

DIRECTIONS

✔ Combine all of the ingredients and toss, making certain that all of the fruit is coated with the mayonnaise.
✔ Cover and refrigerate for eight hours to blend the flavors.

Dessert

Dessert to the modern mind has become an extra; a part of dining that is loaded with forbidden sugars. I can only tell you that to forego a taste treat that signals the last bite of a wonderfully prepared meal appears silly. Eat less dessert, smaller portions appear justified, but take a few dessert recipes, make them your own, and serve them with pride.

The era of a table overflowing with pies, cakes and cookies belongs to a bygone era. The older people in my family would bake cakes, pies and cookies for all of life's events. If a friend passed away, a cake would always be sent to the house; if family, two cakes. If celebrating a birthday for children, then cookies; if for an adult, fruit pies. There were New Year's cakes, Fourth of July pies, Jefferson Davis birthday pies and at Christmas every article of their baking art.

I know from my entertaining that a great dessert is appreciated. But as in all of my cooking, I have taken care to perfect certain recipes that appeal to me, that my guests clammer for and that have been enjoyed in Kentucky for many generations. I choose to offer you desserts that I prepare, and leave the full range of dessert recipes to others.

87. Pie Crust

I often buy a pie shell rather than make a pie-crust pastry from scratch. When I am in a pie-making frame of mind, I make three or four pies at the same time and purchasing the pie-crust pastry eliminates a labor intensive step. And unless I confess my crime of purchasing the pie crust no one seems to care. The insouciance, I believe, derives from the fact that our guests are bereft of a proper comparison. Good pastry cooks in the home are becoming scarce.

But let me tell you, absolutely and unequivocally, a home-made pie crust pastry is worth the fight. A made-from-scratch pie crust is flaky and light and emits that wonderful aroma of fresh-baked bread. I never, ever care if my pie crust is perfectly rolled out or that the rim of my pie is not picture perfect.

My pies will not win a food photography contest. But my guests from adolescence to old age love my pies made with my homemade pie-crust pastry. And for me that is the bag limit.

Store your flour and shortening or oil used for baking in the back of the refrigerator. In making a pie crust it is imperative that you keep the ingredients cold, thereby keeping the dough cool. Put the mixing bowl and the two pastry knives in the refrigerator an hour before use.

And by all means handle the dough as little as possible and roll it out quickly from the middle out, taking care not to roll over the edges.

INGREDIENTS
3 C flour
1/2-t baking powder
1/2-t salt
1 C shorting
6 T ice water

DIRECTIONS

✔ In a mixing bowl sift together the flour, baking powder and salt.

✔ Using the pastry knives scissors fashion, cut the shortening into the flour until it is pebbly. Add the ice water a tablespoon at a time and cut in with the pastry knives.

✔ Using floured hands remove the pastry from the bowl and place on a floured table. Separate the dough into two balls and roll from the center out to 1/4-inch. Each edge should be about 6-inches from the middle of the pastry.

✔ Fold the dough over north to south, then east to west and transport it to a glass pie pan, leaving about a 1/2-inch overhang that you may trim or build up about the rim of the pan. The second pastry ball is rolled out in the same way and either placed atop the pie as a cover or it is cut into strips to crisscross the pie. 4 In either case, press the top pastry edges into the pastry rim with thumb and forefinger. If you choose to cover the pie, cut several slits in the middle of the pie crust to vent the steam.

88. Kentucky Pie

This pie is enjoyed throughout the South and is a Kentucky standard dessert. It is traditionally served sliced, in a small wedge, partnered with vanilla ice cream.

Kentucky Pie is a custard dessert and therefore it does not require a pie crust cover.

INGREDIENTS
1 C pecans, chopped
1/4 C pecans, whole
3 eggs, beaten
6 oz. brown sugar
2 oz. butter, melted
1 T vanilla
1/4-t salt
1 pie crust

DIRECTIONS

✔ Beat eggs in a large bowl. Add in the chopped pecans, brown sugar, butter, vanilla and salt. Stir with a whisk until blended.
✔ Pour the ingredients into the pie crust.
✔ Dot the top of the pie with the whole pecans.
✔ Bake at 350 degrees for 55 minutes. Allow the Kentucky Pie to cool before serving.

89. Chocolate Bourbon Pie

I have had the privilege of eating as many versions of chocolate bourbon pie as there are Kentucky cooks who prepare pies. This recipe has been widely used in central Kentucky and has been a favorite in my family for many generations. I am certain each of us has made the pie to suit our taste but the essence of the pie has always been pecans, bourbon and bittersweet chocolate.

We will make chocolate bourbon pie for any occasion and serve it for dessert at luncheon or dinner. At these meal times it is served warm. The midnight snackers can be counted upon to make a clean sweep of the pie pan, at which time it is consumed at room temperature.

Chocolate bourbon pie is an exceedingly rich dessert. We serve it as a small wedge with strong coffee.

INGREDIENTS
1 pie crust
4 eggs, beaten
1 C corn syrup
3/4 C light brown sugar
1/3 C butter
3 T fine aged Kentucky bourbon whisky
1 T vanilla
1 T flour
6 oz. bittersweet baker's chocolate, chopped into morsel-size pieces
1 C pecans, coarsely chopped

DIRECTIONS

✔ Place the pie crust into a 9" pie plate and fold edges over, pinching the dough around the rim.
✔ In a mixing bowl, using a whisk, blend together the eggs, syrup, sugar and butter.
✔ Add the bourbon, vanilla and flour.
✔ When the mixture is smooth, add the chocolate and the pecans.
✔ Pour the contents of the mixing bowl into the pie crust.
✔ Bake at 350 degrees for 1 hour.

90. Lemon Squares

I love lemon, the more the better. This dessert fits the bill. It is very lemony, very rich and tremendously fattening. But if you can stand it, take a square. Your diet plan goes out of the window. This dessert makes every one feel a little foolish—as your guests will look for a second square to keep company with the lemon square they have just eaten, all the while protesting their indulgence. We serve lemon squares wherever and whenever.

INGREDIENTS
1-1/2 C flour
1/2 C powdered sugar
1-1/2 sticks butter
1/4-t baking powder
3 eggs, beaten
1-1/2 C sugar
4 T lemon juice, fresh squeezed
3 T flour
extra powdered sugar

DIRECTIONS

✔ Place the first four ingredients in a bowl and whisk briskly. Flour your hands and press into a dry baking dish. Bake at 350 degrees for 15 minutes. Set aside.

✔ In a mixing bowl, combine the eggs and the sugar and blend at a medium speed. Add the 3 T of flour and the lemon juice. Then pour the mixture into the crust you have just baked.

✔ Bake at 350 degrees for 25 minutes. Allow the lemon squares to cool, then cover with tin foil and refrigerate for use the next day.

✔ Before serving sprinkle powdered sugar across the top.

"Kentucky"

Kentucky's rolling fields of green,
With bluegrass clothed, I love;
Her sluggish streams and verdant woods,
Her azure sky above.

I love the spirit of her folk –
A spirit known by few
Her gracious hospitality –
As lavish as the dew.

Despite hot feeling running high,
Despite the mountain feud –
Despite Kentucky's lofty pride,
Her people are not rude.

Within her bounds no poor unfed
From home aplenty turn,
But tramping hosts are daily fed –
Her face with shame would burn.

Did hunger go unsatisfied,
When in her plenteous store
Was food enough for every need –
For every need and more.

For things like this thy glory stands,
Kentucky famed in song;
And if these virtues thou dost prove,
Thy sons shall love thee long.

– D. Roy Mathews

91. Chocolate Sauce

"Y'all" listen to Colonel Michael on this recipe. A crowd favorite emanating from the Elmwood kitchen, chocolate sauce is really out of this world. Mimi brought out the chocolate sauce for every occasion. When victories and defeats would be shared within the family circle—chocolate sauce would appear to caress and comfort. The matriarch of Elmwood found chocolate sauce to be the most sought after recipe in her considerable repertory.

When I serve chocolate sauce, my guests, regardless of their age, go to the moon on the first taste of chocolate sauce over plain chocolate cake or vanilla ice cream.

Your friends will request chocolate sauce even if they have not been invited to dinner. However, it is useful to note that the lack of cake or ice cream will not inhibit passion for chocolate sauce. Your friends and family, if they know chocolate sauce is in the kitchen, will eat it with a fork, knife or spoon—be they doctor, lawyer, merchant or thief!

INGREDIENTS
3/4 C evaporated milk
1/2 stick of butter
3/4 C white powdered sugar
3 oz. bitter-sweet baking chocolate
1-t vanilla

DIRECTIONS

✔ In a pan, on a low heat, carefully blend together the milk and the butter.

✔ Add the powdered sugar and stir with the whisk until the sugar is thoroughly dissolved.

✔ Add the chocolate and stir until thoroughly blended. Lightly heat the sauce until very smooth, about 10 minutes. Continuously stir with a whisk, and do not let it simmer or it will stick.

✔ Turn off the heat and add the vanilla, gently stirring it in with the whisk.

✔ Refrigerate after it has cooled Serve warm over plain chocolate cake or vanilla ice cream or anything else you can think of.

92. Orange Bourbon Sauce

Be extra careful around this sauce. It is good. Seriously, this is really delicious. It is interesting that I do not find this sauce outside of central Kentucky. We have made orange bourbon sauce for years. My guests absolutely love it and we continue to find new ways to use it..

I have used it for years on pumpkin pie with great effect. And as previously reported, this sauce works great with cooked carrots.

Pour it over chocolate ice cream or on the top of a cheesecake. On puff-filled dessert pastry it is terrific.

If you cook ducks, geese and pheasants during the holiday season, glaze the birds when they are placed upon the table and leave a serving dish filled with orange bourbon sauce.

INGREDIENTS

1/2 C brown sugar
1/4 C water
1/4 C fine-aged Kentucky bourbon whisky
1/4 C pecans, chopped medium
1/4 C strawberry preserves
1/4 orange, peeled, seeds removed, sliced
1/4 lemon, peeled, seeds removed, sliced
2-t cornstarch

DIRECTIONS

✔ Simmer the brown sugar, and water until dissolved.

✔ Then, add the bourbon whisky, pecans and strawberry preserves, simmer about 2 minutes, stirring with a whisk.

✔ Add the orange and the lemon and the cornstarch and simmer until it is syrup thick. If you feel the sauce needs a little more cornstarch, add a teaspoon or two.

✔ Cover and store in refrigerator overnight to blend the flavors. It is generally served warm but room temperature is fine by me.

93. Bourbon Sauce

This sauce is world class. A good bourbon sauce is in every reputable Kentucky kitchen and every knowledgeable Kentucky cook has a version they lay claim to. We use it on every manner of cake and puff pastry. The two-egg cake with bourbon sauce is perfect. It is also delicious over strawberry and cantaloupe. On blackberry cake it is magnificent.

The bourbon sauce I give you, like the chocolate sauce, came from Mimi, a woman under constant siege. Her family and friends have asked her to reproduce her version of this recipe so often that she finally had it printed and kept a supply in her kitchen office drawer. This dessert topping is a Kentucky classic.

There will never be enough bourbon sauce, for if there is a portion left behind, I assure you, it will go home with somebody. You will get so many requests for it that only in the making of it will you achieve peace.

It has been years since I have seen anyone cook with a double boiler that was specifically manufactured for that purpose. I use two pans that seem to set one on top of the other. Bourbon sauce will not tolerate a lot of heat, if it simmers, it will curdle. I even lift the pan slightly away from the steam as I stir in the egg yolk. Mimi finds this unnecessary but I have always conceded to her the possession of a more assured hand.

INGREDIENTS
1 C sugar
1 stick butter
1 C Half and Half
4 egg yolks, beaten lightly
1 pinch salt
1/2 C fine-aged Kentucky bourbon whisky

DIRECTIONS

✔ In a double boiler, set the water to a light boil. Blend the butter and the sugar into the upper bowl, using a whisk.
✔ Add Half and Half and stir well until dissolved.
✔ Add the egg yolks and salt and stir until thickened.
✔ Add bourbon whisky.
✔ Served lightly warm.

94. Blackberry Bourbon Sauce Cake

McManus House, at various times, is a hotbed of dessert-making activity. The holiday seasons always have dessert interest. But when good old friends arrive upon our doorstep after years of absence, if we ask for a dessert suggestion, they first declare chocolate sauce or bourbon sauce on top of anything, and back it up with a request for blackberry bourbon sauce cake. This cake, I am sure, is as old as Kentucky. I first read a version of it in a cookbook written before the War Between the States.

At Elmwood, Mimi celebrates everyone's birthday, regardless of age, regardless of family surname. If you come to Elmwood for dinner and she either knows or discovers you are in your birthday week, she makes a blackberry bourbon sauce cake. In all of my years, I never, ever heard anyone who wanted any other birthday cake. Good thing: Mimi never offered any other.

In Kentucky, blackberries are everywhere. Before the thornless variety came into our agriculture, we endured the sharp painful scratches associated with pickin' blackberries. To encourage efficient effort, a string was attached to a coffee can, which was hung from our neck so that we could have the use of both hands while pickin' blackberries. No one above the age of six escaped the chore. And except for an occasional yelp or cussin' attack, there were few complaints, though I must say the occasional snake making its presence known elicited colorful and vociferous language with a simultaneous leap out of the blackberry bush. We endured, for we knew at the end of the pickin' torture there would be gallons of blackberry jam, jelly and syrup.

Now, instead of finding the blackberry harvest along the fence-rows and abandoned roadways, I grow a thornless variety in my arbor. My sisters declare I have grown soft as I advance in years.

INGREDIENTS
1/2 C buttermilk
1-t soda
1 C flour, sifted
1-t cinnamon
1 C sugar
1/2 C butter
3 eggs, beaten
1 C blackberry jam (1 C blackberries and 1 C sugar blended at medium speed)

DIRECTIONS

- ✔ **Dissolve the soda into the buttermilk and set aside. Sift the flour with the cinnamon and set aside.**
- ✔ **Using a whisk, blend the butter and sugar in a large mixing bowl. Add the eggs and buttermilk and blend until smooth. Add the flour and blackberry jam and stir well.**
- ✔ **Pour into an oiled shallow 12" baking dish.**
- ✔ **Bake at 325 degrees for 40 minutes. Cut into squares and serve with bourbon sauce.**

"Joy in Old Kentucky," 1906

There is joy in old Kentucky
Where the upland grass is blue
Where the maids are sweet and winning,
Where the hearts of men are true
There is joy in old Kentucky
When the daylight turns to gloam,
For her call has filled the country
And her sons are coming home.

– Anonymous

95. Blueberry-Raspberry Cheesecake

Past generations of my family enthusiastically recalled the making of cheesecake. It had to do with a very laborious effort of beating eggs, butter and milk into a custard then adding flour—passing the resultant brew through cheesecloth and then progressing to the next steps. I can not even think in terms that complicated. As for making my own cream cheese, I have developed no nostalgia for the work.

Blueberry-raspberry cheesecake is a dessert I make when I want to show off. Everyone steers a wide berth around the making of cheesecake because it appears complicated and the spring-form pan is a foreign piece of kitchen equipment. However, if you will relax about the former and purchase the latter, cheesecake is simple to make.

I have often contemplated eating a whole blueberry-raspberry cheesecake by myself. I have never done so, although the thought is invariably with me every time I make it. The women of our clan keep me to one piece of blueberry-raspberry cheesecake and our guests are of no help to me. They love blueberry-raspberry cheesecake as much as I do and the pan is cleaned with their second helpings. Poor me.

INGREDIENTS

1-1/2 C pecans, finely ground
1/4 C sugar
3 T butter
1 T flour
3 8-oz. cartons of Philadelphia cream cheese
1-1/4 C sugar
3 T flour
1 T lemon rind, grated
1/2 T salt
4 eggs, lightly beaten
8 oz. sour cream
1-t vanilla
1 C blueberries
1 C raspberries
1 C whipping cream

DIRECTIONS

✔ Blend together the pecans, sugar, butter and flour. Press this into the bottom of the spring-form pan, allowing this crust to come up the sides about 1 inch.

✔ Using a blender, beat the cream cheese at a medium speed until it is smooth. Add the sugar, flour and salt gradually to be certain the cream cheese is equally covered.

✔ Add the eggs gradually and when completely mixed in, add the sour cream, vanilla and lemon rind. Turn the blender to a slow speed and add the blueberries, raspberries and the whipping cream.

✔ Pour the cheesecake mixture into the spring-form pan.

✔ Bake at 300 degrees for 75 minutes.

96. Pineapple Upside-Down Cake

We will use pineapple upside-down cake for any occasion. It is a traditional cake for weddings and anniversary celebrations. By all means use fresh pineapple. I know the modern way is to use that syrupy version in the can. I simply cannot force myself to use fruit packed that way.

INGREDIENTS

1 stick butter, melted
1 C brown sugar
6 pineapple slices, medium thick
1 two-egg cake batter

DIRECTIONS

✔ Use a black castiron skillet. Pour the butter into skillet, Coat the side of the pan with the butter, up to the rim. Sprinkle the brown sugar on top of the butter that is in the bottom of the skillet. Layer the pineapple slices on top of the brown sugar.

✔ Pour in the batter for the two egg cake.

✔ Bake at 375 degrees for 45-50 minutes.

✔ When you remove the pineapple upside-down cake from the oven, turn the pan over onto a serving plate, using a knife around the skillet sides to extricate the cake.

97. Apple Pie

I do not know of any food in American life that is as important as apple pie. We speak of apple pie in the same breath we pronounce our love for our country and the mother that gave us life. I promise you, if you will cook a good apple pie and are willing to prepare it often, you will be revered among your family and friends.

There are many good recipes for apple pie and it seems each region of the country has a version of apple pie that is dear to them. The common element in every great apple pie recipe is a great tasting pie crust. I am adamant about using a homemade pie-crust pastry in the making of an apple pie. I never take an apple pie seriously that uses a store-bought pie crust. A homemade pie crust has dramatically more flavor and aroma than a commercially-prepared pie crust. And besides, anything that is as emotionally powerful as an apple pie needs to be done right.

INGREDIENTS
2 pie crusts
1 C sugar
1/4 C brown sugar
2 T flour
1-t cinnamon
1-t nutmeg
6 apples, cored, peeled and sliced
1/2 C orange juice
1/2 C butter, softened

DIRECTIONS

✔ Roll out the two pie crusts. Place one of the pie crusts in the pie pan, leaving about 1/2-inch overhang.

✔ Mix together the dry ingredients and sprinkle about a third of it onto the pie crust that is in the pie pan.

✔ Pour in the apples that have been quartered then cut three times.

4 Mix together the orange juice and butter and pour over the apples. Sprinkle the rest of the dry ingredients over the apples.

✔ Cover the pie with the extra pie crust. Cut 3-4 slits in middle of crust. Press the two crusts together by pinching them along the rim.

✔ Bake at 375 degrees for 1 hour.

98. Two-Egg Cake

INGREDIENTS
2-1/2-t baking powder
1/4-t salt
2-1/4 C flour, sifted
1 C sugar
1 stick butter
2 eggs, beaten
3/4 C milk

DIRECTIONS

✔ Sift the flour and the baking powder and salt together, twice. In a mixing bowl on slow speed, cream the sugar and the butter. 4 Add the eggs and the milk. Pour the flour into the mixing bowl, still set on a slow speed, a small amount at a time, making certain that the batter is well blended.

✔ Pour the batter into a baking pan. Bake at 375 degrees for 25 minutes or until the interior of the cake is dry.

99. Bourbon Butter Cream Pie

INGREDIENTS
1 C heavy whipping cream
1 stick plus 6 T butter
4 eggs, beaten lightly
2-1/4 C sugar
2-1/2 T flour
1-t salt
2 T fine aged Kentucky bourbon whisky
1-t vanilla
1 pie crust

DIRECTIONS

✔ Blend the butter, cream in the top of a double boiler, stirring with the whisk. Then add the eggs.

✔ Add in remaining ingredients gradually, stirring constantly

✔ Pour into the unbaked pie crust.

✔ Bake at 325 degrees for 1 hour, shaking the pie gently two times during the hour. Allow the pie to cool and the pie will firm up.

100. Fruit Pies

There are plenty of ways to make a good fruit pie. Some use more or less lemon, fruit, sugar or salt. My advice is to experiment. Fruit pies are delicious almost any way you fix them. I highly recommend that you use a homemade pie crust. The fruit pie will end up looking a bit irregular and imperfect but for me, therein, is the charm. I often use a commercially purchased pie crust for fruit pies as I stand my ground on apple pie and choose not to use the same reverence for fruit pies. The truth be known, few will point out the expediency.

The fruit pies I enjoy are the ones that have survived to the modern kitchen: blueberry, raspberry, blackberry, peach and cherry. I must leave boysenberry, gooseberry and rhubarb pies to the era of my grandparents who remembered these pies fondly but are foreign to my experience.

INGREDIENTS
2 pie crusts
1 C sugar
4 T flour
1/4-t salt
4 C fruit, washed, hulled or stoned
3 T butter
1 T lemon juice

DIRECTIONS

✔ Line the pie pan with a pie crust pastry.

✔ Mix together the sugar, flour and salt and sprinkle about a third onto the pie crust pastry. Pour the fruit into the pie shell. Sprinkle the remainder of the sugar, flour and salt onto the fruit. Dot the fruit with the butter and the lemon juice.

✔ Crisscross the top of the pie or cover the pie with the extra pie crust.

✔ Bake at 425 degrees for 45-55 minutes. Allow to cool before serving.

101. Kentucky Flaming Peaches

A formal dinner for six seated at the table of McManus House on a cold blustery night in February requires flaming peaches for dessert. The peaches are served over vanilla ice cream accompanied by the warm blue blaze of the brandy.

Margaret Sue and her friends like chocolate sauce over the peaches. I have never thought the chocolate sauce necessary, as the Kentucky flaming peaches are so good by themselves. However, I have chosen to decline battle on this issue as I have always deemed it wise to bow to the dessert preferences of women.

INGREDIENTS

3 C water
1 1/2 C sugar
2-t vanilla
1 lemon rind, grated
1 C strawberry jam
8 peaches, skinned, stoned and thin sliced
1/4 C fine aged Kentucky bourbon whisky
vanilla ice cream
chocolate sauce, if you must
2/3 C brandy

DIRECTIONS

✔ The peaches are cut and the dessert mixture is made up in the pan they will cook in prior to the dinner. After dinner bring the dessert mixture almost to a boil. Simmer for about a minute, stirring with a whisk.

✔ Add the peaches and the bourbon to the pan and stir in just prior to serving.

✔ Place the ice cream in large scoops into a silver or formal glass-serving bowl and pour the peaches on top of the ice cream. 4 If you are going to add chocolate sauce, this is the time to do it. Carry the bowl to the table along with a glass of brandy.

✔ Pour the brandy into a long handled silver ladle, ignite the brandy and quickly pour the flaming brandy onto the peaches. Serve the dessert just as the flames disappear.

102. Pumpkin Pie

INGREDIENTS
2 C Half and Half
1-1/2 C pumpkin, canned
1/2 C brown sugar
1-t cinnamon
1/2-t nutmeg
1/2-t salt
2 eggs, beaten
1 pie crust
nutmeg

DIRECTIONS
✔ In a bowl, mix all of the ingredients completely. Pour the pumpkin mixture into the pie shell.
✔ Place a pie crust into a pie pan. Create a rim on the pie pan if you like.
✔ Bake at 375 degrees for 30-40 minutes and allow to cool. Sprinkle the top with nutmeg.

103. Strawberry Shortcake

In the late spring just as southern winds warm the Kentucky soil, strawberries ripen and the competition to harvest this luscious fruit begins with a passion and a fury. From mid-May to mid-June the outcome is decided on a daily basis. Birds love red ripe strawberries. I can usually beat my avian adversary to the berry patch as they do not roust from their slumbers until just before dawn. To the consternation of Margaret Sue, I am in the spring garden before first light.

I like a strawberry in any form it is presented to me. Strawberry shortcake is a capital way to enjoy this fruit. The amount of sugar used in this dessert is strictly personal. If I thought I could avert a riot I would delete the powdered sugar as I find the strawberries sweet enough. Whipped cream is mandatory.

INGREDIENTS
1/2 C sugar
2 C cake flour, sifted
4-t baking powder
1/2-t salt
2 T sugar
6 T shortening
1 egg, beaten
1/2 C whole milk
2 T butter, softened
powdered sugar
whipped cream, chilled
4 C strawberries, crushed then chilled

DIRECTIONS

✔ Make the shortcake. In a mixing bowl sift all of the dry ingredients together.

✔ Cut in the shortening with pastry knives until it is pebbly. Then cut in the egg and milk.

✔ Turn the dough out onto a floured table and knead 10 times turning the dough into itself each time.

✔ Roll out the dough to 1/2-inch, spread on the butter and fold the dough in half, pressing the edges together with the rolling pin.

✔ Cut the dough with a 3-inch biscuit cutter and place the shortcake rounds on a greased baking sheet.

✔ Bake at 450 degrees for about 12 minutes or until a light brown.When cool, place a single shortcake round on a dessert plate.

✔ In a mixing bowl crush the strawberries with a fork and set in the refrigerator to cool.

✔ Open the shortcake round and ladle in the crushed strawberries, then ladle some on top.

✔ Place whole strawberries next to the shortcake. Sprinkle the strawberries with powdered sugar and spoon on whipped cream.

Libation

Wherever I have traveled in the world, and when I proclaim I am from Kentucky, I am immediately told that our Commonwealth is known for fast horses, bourbon whisky and beautiful women. I always heartily agree and add "for chivalrous men too!" They glaze over on that remark.

But when talking about a good drink, it is Kentucky bourbon whisky that captures my interest. There are many good bourbon whiskies distilled in Kentucky and a few great ones. It has a lot to do with individual tastes. I am enthusiastically partial to Breeder's Preference, my family's bourbon whisky, while recognizing that it is a small production bourbon whisky that is not for sale.

Even though I feel a great Kentucky kinship with bourbon whisky, I stock a variety of liquors and drinks for the enjoyment of our guests. A well-stocked bar for McManus House means that we will be prepared to mix about two dozen drinks typically called for in the Commonwealth and across the South. Our bar offers bourbon, gin, scotch, dark rum, vodka, a sweet white wine, a burgundy wine, beer, soft drinks and iced tea.

We set the bar up with orange juice, cranberry juice, tonic, soda and bitters. Lemon and lime, fresh cut, are in their bowls. A jar each of maraschino cherries, cocktail onions and green olives are made available. A pitcher of water and a chest full of ice are at hand. We like to place out about double the amount of short and tall glasses as there are guests, for those either desiring a fresh glass or having misplaced the one they recently carried. Cocktail napkins are in good supply.

In formal dining we will serve a wine that complements the entrée. After dinner liqueurs are served in small snifters to reflect our notion that the evening is drawing to a close.

In every community there are men and women whom you can employ to help in the task of tending the bar. Find a man or woman who enjoys mixing drinks; if you can find someone who has a great personality, all the better. A good bartender is a part of the social occasion, and the man that comes when I call, I consider a friend. I always make certain that the bartender receives a generous plate of the foods we have prepared. They appreciate the courtesy, and after all, they too are at the party.

104. Bourbon—Straight

Straight bourbon over ice is the drink of choice with our crowd. Bourbon is a uniquely Kentucky whisky, enjoyed throughout the world. It is a drink that finds itself in the company of our family and good friends.

Bourbon straight. It simply does not get any better than this.

Pack a short tumbler glass with cubed ice. Pour a jigger of fine aged Kentucky bourbon whisky into the glass. Allow the bourbon and the ice to get acquainted for about a minute. Raise the glass. Smell the bouquet. Sip fine aged Kentucky bourbon whisky.

105. Bourbon—Toddy

Pack crushed ice into an old fashioned or tumbler glass. Add 1 teaspoon of sugar, a jigger of fine aged Kentucky bourbon whisky and a twist of lemon. Fill the glass with water. Stir briskly with a bar spoon. Put in a mint cherry.

106. Bourbon—Old Fashioned

Make the Toddy minus the mint cherry and add a maraschino cherry, and a dash of Angostura bitters. Place a slice of lemon and orange on the rim of the glass.

107. Bourbon—Moon Glow

The Moon Glow is a potion I made up and finds favor with the gentlewomen. Watch this one. It will sneak up on you. It is so good that my friends press me to make them. Our bartender, who assists us in our home, is kept busy mixing the Moon Glow.

Pack a tall glass with crushed ice. Fill half the glass with equal parts cranberry and orange juice. Add 2 teaspoons of maraschino cherry juice. Pour in a jigger of fine-aged Kentucky bourbon whisky. Stir well with the bar spoon. Drop in 2 maraschino cherries. Place a straw in the drink.

108. Bourbon – Sour

Pack a cocktail shaker with cracked ice. Squeeze the juice of 1/2 of a lemon onto the ice. Add 1/2 teaspoon of sugar. Pour in a jigger of fine-aged Kentucky bourbon whisky. Shake well. Uncover and add a spillage of club soda into the shaker. Using a strainer, pour the whisky sour into a tumbler glass. Drop in a maraschino cherry and place a slice of orange on the rim of the glass.

109. Bourbon – Mint Julep

The mint julep has long been associated with Kentucky in general and with the Kentucky Derby in particular. The Kentucky Derby is a truly international horse race that takes place at Churchill Downs in Louisville on the first Saturday in May of each year. The mint julep is a celebration of the springtime racing season in Kentucky.

Take your time in making the mint julep. Embodied in this drink is a taste of old Kentucky. The mint julep is a drink that we prepare throughout the summer, usually for out of town guests.

Use a silver julep cup when you can, as it frosts well and is part of the Kentucky tradition. Use a highball glass if you find yourself without a silver julep cup; it will not frost well, but it will do.

Take a sprig of mint and rub it around the inside of the julep cup, exerting a gentle pressure. Place this sprig of mint in a napkin and reverently dispose of it, for the mint has performed its service.

Place the crushed ice in the julep cup to the brim. Place the julep cup in the freezer for about an hour.

In a bowl place a tablespoon of sugar for each anticipated call for the mint julep. Pour in enough water to cover the sugar and stir until the sugar is dissolved. Collect about six sprigs of mint per julep and with a firm pressure from a wooden pestle crush the mint into the syrup mixture.

Retrieve the julep cup from the freezer with a napkin so as not to break the frost that has formed on the julep cup. Pour in a half tablespoon of the syrup, while holding back the crushed mint. Add 2 jiggers of fine-aged Kentucky bourbon whisky. Mix gently with a bar spoon. Decorate the julep with two sprigs of mint and a dash of powdered sugar. Place a straw into the julep cup that is sized to peer just over the rim. Serve immediately.

And, oh by the way, please cleanse the bowl containing the syrup with a fresh napkin, so as to capture the mint for disposal. There are two centuries of tradition in making the mint julep. We always try to act nobly toward our friends.

110. Scotch – Straight

I have a fondness for a good Scotch whisky, in the same way I enjoy my old friends who reside in distant regions. In my opinion there is only one way to enjoy Scotch whisky and that is straight, over ice, in a small tumbler glass. Some of my friends enjoy scotch in a tall glass with soda water.

111. Gin – Dry Martini

The classic dry martini is made by the silver pitcher packed with cracked ice and is 2/3 dry gin, 1/3 vermouth, 1 dash Angostura bitters for each jigger of dry gin. Stir with a bar spoon and using a strainer pour into the dry martini glass or a tumbler glass. I have always disliked seeing a good dry martini beaten to death by ice in a shaker and so gravitate toward the pitcher and the stir stick.

If making a single dry martini without the use of a strainer, pack a tumbler glass with cracked or crushed ice. Pour in a jigger of dry gin, 1/2 capful of vermouth and a dash of Angostura bitters. Stir.

Either way, add 2 green olives for the dry martini, use 2 cocktail onions in place of the olives to create the Gibson martini.

112. Gin—Gin and Tonic

There is always a place for this very popular warm weather drink. Pack a tall glass with ice cubes. Pour a jigger of dry gin and fill the glass with tonic water. Squeeze a quarter of a lemon or lime into the drink and toss in the fruit. Delightful.

113. Gin—Tom Collins

This is my favorite gin drink with club soda. I do not see much call for it in this modern era but it is excellent. Put 3 cubes of ice into a tall glass. Squeeze 1/2 of a lime onto the ice. Add 1 teaspoon of powdered sugar. Pour in a jigger of dry gin and fill the glass with club soda. Stir briskly with a bar spoon.

114. Gin—Screwdriver

A truly great summertime drink for the late afternoon. Pack a tall glass with ice cubes. Pour in a jigger of dry gin. Fill the glass with fresh squeezed orange juice. Stir briskly. Squeeze a quarter of a lime into the drink and toss in the fruit but do not stir, just enjoy.

115. Gin—Gin Alexander

Margaret Sue and her friends love to drink this cocktail at the racetrack. The recipe I used for years called for cream but I find our crowd likes vanilla ice cream more, so that is the version I give you. I feel protective of Margaret Sue's well being when she calls for a Gin Alexander. She never feels like she is partaking of a drink that sports alcohol. Mix a pitcher half full with 1/3 dry gin, 1/3 Cream de Cacao and 1/3 softened vanilla ice cream. Add crushed ice to within an inch of the pitcher rim. Shake well and strain the mixture into a cocktail glass. Brandy is a popular substitute for the gin.

116. Gin—Champagne Delight I

This is a very flavorful drink for the ladies of the house who like a sweet drink with an attitude. Make the champagne punch in a glass pitcher with 2/3 dry gin, 1/3 lemon juice and 1 teaspoon of powdered sugar for each glass of punch. Stir until you are certain the powdered sugar is dissolved. Fill a champagne glass with crushed ice. Fill the glass half way with the punch, and pour champagne to the rim.

117. Gin – Champagne Delight II

Fill a champagne glass with crushed ice. Add a dash of dry gin, a dash of Angostura bitters, a teaspoon of sugar, stir and fill the glass with champagne. Add a piece of lemon peel for effect.

118. Vodka – Bloody Mary

The classic Bloody Mary mixture made from scratch is 2 jiggers tomato juice, 1/3 jigger lemon juice, 4 dashes of Worcestershire sauce, 1 dash of salt and 1 dash of pepper. The Bloody Mary pre-mix seems to be moreover used, however. Either way, we moisten the rim of a tall glass then upend it, pressing the rim into a small mound of salt. We then pack the glass with cubed ice, add a jigger of vodka and fill the glass with the Bloody Mary ingredient. The contents of the glass are then stirred briskly. We then squeeze 1/4 of a lime into the glass and discard the fruit.

119. Vodka – Vodka Split

The Vodka Split is a drink that is a staple at McManus House and is a drink the women in the Bluegrass invented, as far as I know. I veer around the Vodka Split as a matter of male pride but in all honesty, it is a very good drink. Pack a tall glass with ice cubes. Pour in a jigger of vodka. Fill the glass half way with cranberry juice, then fill the remainder of the glass with fresh squeezed orange juice. Stir. Squeeze a quarter of a lemon on top, discard the fruit and place a fresh slice of lemon on the rim.

"My Old Kentucky Home"

When I came within her borders,
A deeper feeling grew
For the words set to music
That had thrilled me through and through.

Now when I have left her borders,
I've a stronger feeling still,
And the music of that chorus
Ne'er fails my heart to thrill.

Old Kentucky, Old Kentucky!
Once again to see thy face,
To hear the rippling of thy waters –
To be clasped in thy embrace!

Though beyond thy sight and hearing
I'm an exile forced to roam,
Still my heart shall always hearken
To My Old Kentucky Home.

– **Karl D. Kelly**

120. Vodka – Screwdriver and Dry Martini

Follow the recipe for a gin Screwdriver and Dry Martini using vodka.

121. Vodka – Daiquiri

Pack a cocktail shaker with crushed ice. Place the juice of a whole lime into the shaker along with a heaping teaspoon of powdered sugar. Add 1 jigger of vodka. Shake well and strain the daiquiri into a cocktail glass.

122. Iced Tea

Iced tea is enjoyed at all of our warm weather social functions. The way I make the iced tea is very popular. In a two-quart sauce pan, I bring 2 quarts of water to a furious boil. I put three times the normal ration of tea bags into the pan, cut off the heat and allow the tea to steep for three minutes and no more. I then pour the tea into my two quart pitcher, pressing the tea bags to extract the last of the tea essence.

This part is critical. I would not pack the pitcher with ice and pour the freshly steeped tea into the pitcher. I pour the tea from the pitcher into a tall glass packed with cubed ice. This allows each glass of tea poured, to be treated equally by the ice.

A quarter of lemon is squeezed into the glass and the fruit tossed in. Sugar or sweetener is added to taste. The tea then receives a few stirs. A sprig or two of mint is placed inside the rim of the glass, resulting in a refreshing cool drink.

When I can take the time, we place the tea in a covered gallon jar and place it on the rail of the porch to gather the sunlight for an hour. It is an old southern custom to treat the tea this way and I like it.

When I am ensconced at McManus House and when I re-pour a glass of iced tea, I use a fresh glass, replacing the ice and reestablishing the tea, lemon, mint and sugar/sweetener. I do not like to see my recently enjoyed glass of iced tea trying to keep up with a new batch of tea splashed down upon it, thereby, requiring additional flavoring. I never have been a fan of creating a lemon and mint compost heap settling to the bottom of my glass.

"My Old Kentucky Home"

I've wandered in ice covered regions,
Where the mountains mock the stars,
I've mushed through the snows of Alaska
By the light of the Northern Bars;
I've traveled the sands of the desert'
Where the sun turns earth to hell,
I've poled to the source of the Congo,
And gone up the Ganges as well;
I've wandered for years in China,
And followed the life of the sea,
Wherever was war or excitement,
I was almost sure to be.
But no matter the land or country,
By forest or plain or foam,
I have never seen the equal of
"My Old Kentucky Home."

I've listened to music and poetry,
By the savage and Europe's best,
I've read from the masters in England,
And the Indian chants in the West;
I've sung the Italian love songs,
And the music of sunny Spain,
I've couched at the savage tom-tom,
And danced to the bagpipe strain;
I've learned the songs of the desert,
And the chants of the heathen priest,
Both the music of cultured Europe
And the songs of the barbarous East;
I've heard the world's best music,
In forest, or templed dome,
But I've never heard the equal of
"My Old Kentucky Home."

I've met the men of the Races,
The White, the Yellow, the Red,

I've bunked with the western cowboy,
Or sat by his fireside instead;
I've bargained with Chinese merchants,
And fought with the treacherous blacks,
I've met men on highway and byway,
In cities, or wilderness tracts;
I've known them as few others know them,
At work, at war, or at play,
And learned their strength and their weakness,
Until I know when I say;
"In all the world, in all the lands,
Through which I've chanced to roam,
I've never heard the equal of
'My Old Kentucky Home,'"

—Hamilton H. Roberts
Copyrighted 1914

""A Kentucky Toast"

Here's to Old Kentucky,
The State where I was born,
Where the corn is full of kernals,
And the Colonels full of "corn."

—Anonymous

Comments

I have written this book for the gentleman in particular and for gentlewomen generally who enjoy entertaining their family and friends in an atmosphere of simple elegance. No one has the time anymore to learn the cooking and baking arts, and increasingly no one really wants to prepare foods that our science tells us should be sharply reduced or avoided altogether.

And yet we want to entertain in a way that brings honor to our house and pleases our guests. I do not like to employ catering companies or cooks for hire. I find that when people feel insecure about their cooking skill, and feel they must retain catering, that they, as often as not, forego having people over. Besides, a catering company or a cook for hire, even when acceptable, rarely does it to your complete satisfaction. When the caterer prepares the foods you have ordered, somehow, rarely, does it have the taste you anticipated.

I advocate learning twenty outstanding recipes and making them your own by continuous use. In past days, men have been left out of the entertaining equation. The ladies of the house have gravitated to the kitchen, thereby pushing the men into the great outdoors or to an interior den. That is changing, as most of the women I know, get a big kick out of having the man of the house preparing their signature dish. I enjoy cooking for our social occasions, whether large or small, but to my wife's irritation I seem to look to her for the daily and routine cooking chores, except for grilling. I like the fun part, not the routine part of cooking.

In Kentucky we have a long history of entertaining in our homes. We may have memberships in clubs but we have preferred our homes for entertaining. Kentucky's low population density has allowed many of us spacious lawns. Our old tradition of gathering for a spring, summer or fall social occasion on the lawn has allowed us to host rather sizable breakfasts, luncheons and dinners. I entertain outdoors at McManus House in the three warm seasons and then head for the house in winter for more formal entertaining, with fireplaces lit and ready.

The Grand Creator allows most of us only seventy-five or eighty years upon the earth. Enjoy them. And, along the way, learn twenty great recipes and cook them for a lifetime. For your effort you will be renowned as an excellent cook, a great host and if you wish, a Kentucky gentleman or a Kentucky gentlewoman.

The recipes in this collection are based in the Kentucky tradition of hospitality and fine entertaining. Again, the dishes I have included are ones that I use for our social occasions. These dishes are as good in Kentucky as they are elsewhere. If you enjoy cooking and entertaining this book has been written for you.

I have known many of the illustrious writers and food editors that have graced our Commonwealth and this Union with their journalism and flair. I am not in their class. I am a host who enjoys that role. I cook for my family and friends. If they have enjoyed being in my home, being a part of the way in which we entertain, then I am a contented Kentucky gentleman.

If nothing else, learn to cook Beef Masters, make chocolate sauce, serve peeled tomatoes with smearcase, prepare Masters Steak Sauce, have a Derby party on the 1st Saturday in May and discover fine aged Kentucky bourbon whisky.

"And To All, Goodnight"

Yet we have hopes that are immortal – interests that are imperishable – principles that are indestructible. Encouraged by these hopes, stimulated by these interests, and sustained by and sustaining those principles, let us, come to what may, be true to God, true to ourselves, and faithful to our children, our country, and mankind. And, then, whenever or wherever it may be our doom to look, for the last time, on earth, we may be justly proud of the title of "Kentuckian," and, with our expiring breath, may cordially exclaim:
Kentucky as she was – Kentucky as she is –
Kentucky as she will be – Kentucky forever!

– George Robertson

Index

Entrées

Vegetables

Pick Up Foods

Breads

Meat/Vegetable Sauces and Salad Dressings

Salads

Dessert

Libation

The Colonel's Cottage

The Colonel's Cottage

114 South Fourth Street, Bardstown, KY 40004
1-800-704-4917
www.thecolonelscottage.com

The Colonel's Cottage is an inn for couples on a romantic getaway. It is a private, unhosted bed and breakfast across the street from the pioneer park, in Bardstown's downtown historic district. The Colonel's Cottage is reserved by an individual or a couple who have the entire inn to themselves throughout their stay.

The residence was built in 1850 and is in the Federalist style of cottage architecture. The high ceilings and their broad crown moldings are spectacular. The cottage is furnished in Kentucky antiques and furniture reflecting the period prior to the War Between the States.

The Colonel's Cottage has a beautiful living room with fireplace, a stunning dining room, two bedrooms and two baths, one of which is a spa with wonderful cherry woodwork and a double whirlpool bath for all-season relaxation.

Simply Elegant Cooking and Entertaining

"Colonel Masters provides his hospitality to the most important people in his life – his family and friends. I will remember the times we spent at his house for the rest of my life. His entertaining is laced with the power of his hospitality and his great Kentucky cuisine."

– **Margaret Cornett Simms,**
Atlanta, Georgia